PRAISE FOR

"Avrom Sutzkever has no more loving translator than fellow poet Richard Fein. Even those who think they 'do not understand poetry' will be inspired by the poet who bore witness to the most dramatic points of modern Jewish experience and could transmit their power. Strength and spirit fuse in Sutzkever, wit and insight, moral confidence and grace. Our thanks to the translator and to Justin Cammy's introduction for bringing this Jewish cultural landmark to English readers."

— Ruth R. Wisse, author of *No Joke: Making Jewish Humor*

"Richard Fein's translations strive for the impossible acrobatics of Sutzkever's writing, from the rare alchemy of his striking metaphors to a postwar longing for poetic redemption in the face of destruction. To capture just an echo of Sutzkever's singular voice would be an achievement. This collection, simultaneously careful and daring in its choices, amplifies that echo to the maximum that the English language would allow."

— Saul Noam Zaritt, Harvard University

"In dialogue with Avrom Sutzkever, Richard Fein offers us a vibrant selection of the poet's works in a beautiful facing-page translation. Sutzkever's superbly inventive Yiddish imagery and wordcraft inspired Fein, the poet-translator, to dynamically engage both Yiddish and English, with remarkable and moving results."

— Ellen Kellman, Brandeis University

ALSO BY RICHARD J. FEIN

POETRY

PROSE

THE FULL POMEGRANATE

SUNY series in Contemporary Jewish Literature and Culture

Ezra Cappell, editor

———————————————————————

Dan Shiffman, *College Bound:*
The Pursuit of Education in Jewish American Literature, 1896–1944

Eric J. Sundquist, editor, *Writing in Witness: A Holocaust Reader*

Noam Pines, *The Infrahuman: Animality in Modern Jewish Literature*

Oded Nir, *Signatures of Struggle:*
The Figuration of Collectivity in Israeli Fiction

THE FULL POMEGRANATE

Poems of Avrom Sutzkever

Selected and translated by
RICHARD J. FEIN

Introduction by
JUSTIN CAMMY

Preparation of the Yiddish text by
HARRY BOCHNER and
DAVID BRAUN

excelsior editions

AN IMPRINT OF STATE UNIVERSITY OF NEW YORK PRESS

Cover art: Benstie Mikhtom, *Avrom Sutzkever* (late 1930s). Published in a folio by members of the literary group Yung-Vilne in honor of Yefim Yeshurin, Vilna, 1939.

Published by State University of New York Press, Albany

Excelsior Editions is an imprint of State University of New York Press

For information, contact State University of New York Press, Albany, NY
www.sunypress.edu

Library of Congress Cataloging-in-Publication Data

Names: Sutzkever, Avrom author | Fein, Richard J. translator
Title: The full pomegranate : poems of of Avrom Sutzkever / Avrom Sutzkever, author.
Description: Albany : State University of New York Press, [2019] | Series: SUNY series in Contemporary Jewish Literature and Culture | Includes bibliographical references and index.
Identifiers: ISBN 9781438472508 (paperback : alk. paper) | ISBN 9781438472515 (e-book)
Further information is available at the Library of Congress.

10 9 8 7 6 5 4 3 2 1

for **SOLON BEINFELD**

who teaches me how to read and translate Yiddish poetry

"like the original poet, the translator is a Narcissus who in this case chooses to contemplate his own likeness not in the spring of nature but in the pool of art."

—RENATO POGGIOLI, "The Added Artificer"

CONTENTS

NOTE ON SELECTION AND ARRANGEMENT

THIS BOOK IS NOT A COMPREHENSIVE OR REPRESENTATIVE selection of the poetry of Avrom Sutzkever. I included here only those poems of his that, over my years of reading him, have said translate me. Thus, this is not a "Selected Poems," but a gathering of Sutzkever's work, from the first to the last volume, that I have needed to get into the language in which I write my own poems.

The earliest poems follow the ordering in *Collected Poems* (*Poetishe verk*), a two-volume edition published in 1963; the rest follow the orderings in the volumes from which they are taken.

When a date or a place name appears at the bottom of a poem it was put there by Sutzkever. The dates sectioning the poems in *Twin Brother* follow Sutzkever's own arrangement, in conformation to the book's subtitle, *Poems from a Diary*. When Sutzkever did not title a poem or if the poem is excerpted from a longer work, I supply a title from the first line of the poem for the table of contents.

NOTE ON TRANSLATION

WHILE MANY OF SUTZKEVER'S POEMS ARE DIRECT AND clear, the main difficulty in translating Sutzkever's poetry is its compact, sometimes dense, syntax. I have not tried to emulate this, finding that such an effort doesn't work in English and is not to my own humor. I have, though, kept his penchant for compound words as much as possible. What I have kept close to are his startling imagery and daring metaphors, which create dramatic, even visionary, psychological effects. It is not his well-known occasional surrealist tendencies that I have striven for as much as what I call the dramatic imagination that crystallizes his poems, his fecund sense of what metaphor can achieve, and how it works in his poems.

I was impelled to translate him; his Yiddish wanted me to find new powers in my English. So, the final poem here, "Sporadic visitant . . .," is fully mine and a testament to my time spent with Avrom Sutzkever.

ACKNOWLEDGMENTS

TERESA IVERSON, GEORGE KALOGERIS AND MARCIA KARP have gone over my translations, sympathetically prodding me to do better. And I want to express my further gratitude to Marcia Karp for preparing a prospectus for the book, which enabled me to find a publisher. Her editorial keenness was of great value. And thanks to Harry Bochner and David Braun for helping me sharpen my translations. Harry Bochner was a lifesaver in the preparation of the Yiddish texts. I also wish to thank Lillian Leavitt for her preparation of the manuscript and our spirited discussion of Sutzkever's poetry.

I am also indebted to Ruth Wisse for granting me permission to publish my translations and the Yiddish originals. Her support has meant a great deal to me. Thanks to Catherine Madsen, of the Yiddish Book Center, who enabled me to obtain copies of Sutzkever's books. Finally, the sketch of Sutzkever on the cover, by Bentsie Mikhtom, was provided by Justin Cammy, and the photograph of Sutzkever for the frontispiece was supplied by Ruth Wisse. I thank the both of them for these images and further thank Justin for writing the introduction and for his advice. I profited from the professionalism and patience of Rafael Chaiken and Jenn Bennett-Genthner of SUNY Press.

Some of the translations in this book were previously published in the following journals and books:

B'KLYN (BrickHouse Books)
    "Granite Wings"
    "Denkmol nokh a ferd"

In geveb: all of *Siberia*

Mudfish: earlier versions of three sections from *Siberia*

My Hands Remember (BrickHouse Books)
    "From Both Ends of the World"
    "It belongs to me"
    "Ever since my pious mother"
    "From a Lost Poem"

Poetry International: "Firefighters"

With Everything We've Got (Host Publications)
    "Ant Nest"
    "Tell"
    "Pasternak"
    "The Woman of Marble in Père Lachaise"
    "Gather Me"
    "To the Thin Vein on My Head"
    "Deer by the Red Sea"
    "So how come?"
    "Poem without a Name"

INTRODUCTION

Justin Cammy

I OWE MY CAREER TO AVROM SUTZKEVER. HE WAS MY LIVING link to what Lucy Dawidowicz referred to as "that place and time," a world in which one's expression of Jewishness and one's engagement with the world were synonymous with the project of building modern Yiddish culture. In the summer of 1994, when I called on Sutzkever in his modest apartment on Moshe Sharett Street in Tel Aviv after having spent a semester studying his work at McGill University, he was excited to learn about the questions that animated the newest generation of Yiddish studies scholars. Though he was not in the best of health, our conversation about his earliest years as a poet in Vilna energized him in ways that enlivened me even more. He leaned forward in his chair when discussing the antics of his colleagues in the literary group Yung-Vilne and young love consummated over books and strolls along the Viliye River. How strange, I remember thinking about myself then, to feel as if I had been born too late. By all rational measures, I was the fortunate one, raised in the freedom of Canada with the privilege of never knowing the humiliations, terrors, and ultimately mass murder that ended the first stage of Sutzkever's career in interwar Poland. However, Sutzkever possessed something that neither I nor most of my contemporaries in North America had: birth into a Jewish language. Having come to my advanced study of Yiddish and Hebrew belatedly, I learned from Sutzkever and his contemporaries that there was something deeply compelling about engaging in dialogue with the world from the perspective of one's own national languages and culture. Sutzkever might have sensed this himself when he handed me his newest volume with the Yiddish inscription "For my young friend Cammy," ending with a doodle of a self-portrait and a self-confident flourish of a signature. His career was marked at various moments by his role as a mentor, and I appreciated this encouraging gesture. As it happens, I went on after that summer to dedicate my graduate studies to the study of Sutzkever and his literary generation, an environment I refer to elsewhere as "when Yiddish was young." The news of his death almost sixteen years later affected me in ways that I could not have expected, as if my own youth had ended with him. I had now matured into a scholarly generation responsible for interpretation and transmission of a cultural and literary legacy that could no longer rely on him as its living standard bearer.

Sutzkever's birth on the eve of World War I in the Yiddish-speaking heartland of Lithuanian Jewry and his death in the Hebrew metropolis of Tel Aviv in 2010 are symbolic of the dramatic geographic, linguistic, and cultural shifts experienced by Eastern European Jews in the twentieth century. Sutzkever's career spanned an interwar secular Yiddish culture unprecedented in its creative scope and geographic range, its destruction at the hands of two totalitarian regimes, the dispersion of its remnants, and a commitment to its regeneration amid a completely transformed postwar Jewish landscape. Though Yiddish literature was blessed with many important writers who came of age at a time marked both by modernist accomplishment and broad popular appeal, few managed to combine Sutzkever's self-assurance as a champion of poetic aestheticism with as dramatic a biography and sense of national responsibility for the postwar fate of Yiddish culture. In the course of a writing career of more than seven decades, he authored more than two dozen poetic volumes, several volumes of surrealist fiction, and a prose memoir of his time in the Vilna ghetto, while for almost half a century *Di goldene keyt* (*The Golden Chain*), the literary journal he founded and edited in Tel Aviv, was the leading international quarterly for discussion and analysis of Yiddish letters.

Sutzkever's importance, of course, is not only measured by his productivity and longevity but by the singularity and universality of his voice. He was the last Yiddish neoromantic, and as such his poetry was marked from its earliest articulations by a fascination with nature, wonder at existence, and celebration of the creative process. As a young writer in Vilna in the 1930s Sutzkever was criticized for privileging art over the context in which it is produced. Though history would later impose itself upon him, first as a poet and memoirist of the Vilna ghetto and later as one of the most refined Yiddish voices to explore the rebirth of the Jewish people in the Land of Israel, he fiercely privileged the aesthetic integrity of the poem itself over any prosaic cause it might serve. Sutzkever liberated Yiddish poetry from the cacophonous politics of the Jewish street while setting for himself the task of crafting a poetic idiom that seemed protoliturgical in its groping for new ways to experience contact with eternity. Moreover, as a consummate master of Yiddish form, rhythm, musicality, and inventive wordplay, he was deeply influenced by the experimental New York writers of the Yiddish introspectivist movement *Inzikh*, with whom he shared the belief that the Jewishness of a Yiddish poet was not necessarily to be found in his subject matter but rather in the organic expression of the poet's relationship with Yiddish as artistic instrument. Sutzkever's *yidishkayt* is predicated, then, on the evident joy he takes in exploring the creative potential of the Yiddish word itself, and pushing the boundaries of the language's prosody. Even after returning to witness the complete destruction of Vilna his primary allegiance to the sacredness of the Yiddish word and its conjuring powers remained unchanged: "I love the unadulterated taste of a word that won't betray itself, / not some sweet-and-sour hybrid with a strange taste. / Whether I rise on the rungs of my ribs, or fall— / that word is mine. A tongue burns in the black pupil of my eye. / No matter how great my generation might be— greater yet is its smallness. / Still eternal is the word in all of its ugliness and splendor." ("To the Thin Vein on My Head," 1945).

AVROM (ABRAHAM) SUTZKEVER WAS BORN JULY 15, 1913 IN Smorgon, an industrial town half way between Vilna and Minsk (then part of late tsarist Russia, today in Belarus), the youngest child of Herts and Reyne Sutzkever. His maternal grandfather was the author of a widely respected rabbinic treatise, part of Lithuanian Jewry's elite tradition of Torah scholarship. His father inherited a local leather goods factory but modeled the *Litvak* commitment to diligent study in his spare time. In 1915, the Jewish residents of Smorgon were falsely accused of espionage and ordered to leave their homes and businesses within twenty-four hours. The Sutzkevers sought refuge in the east, stopping first in Minsk before being encouraged to go on to Omsk, a city on the Irtysh River in southwestern Siberia. Though comparatively safe from the ravages of a continental war that caught large numbers of Eastern European Jews in its crosshairs, the family struggled with poverty, food shortages, an unfamiliar climate, civil war, and Herts Sutzkever's declining health, which prevented him from sustained work. What the Sutzkevers lacked in material security they compensated for in spiritual community by transforming the modest family home in exile into a local intellectual salon. In his later poetry, he often credited his father, who entertained the family on his fiddle, and his older sister Etl, who was a promising poet, as important creative influences. His father's sudden death from a heart attack in Siberia in 1922, and his sister's subsequent death from meningitis in 1925, prompted Sutzkever to return to them often in his writing by situating himself as the inheritor of their artistic potential.

After returning to find the family home in Smorgon in ruins, Sutzkever's widowed mother moved with her children to Vilna (Yiddish Vilne, Polish Wilno), a city recently incorporated into the new Polish republic. According to local Jewish legend, Napoleon had been so impressed with its many establishments of Jewish learning that he referred to it as the Jerusalem of Lithuania. Vilna had a pedigree as a leading center of rabbinic scholarship, home in the eighteenth century to the Vilna Gaon and the proud center of Lithuanian Jewry's rationalist resistance to the spiritual excesses of Hasidism. By the nineteenth century Vilna was a major center for the publication of both traditional religious texts and the modern (secular) Hebrew and Yiddish literatures that were beginning to emerge. As the birthplace of the Jewish socialist Bund and an influential center of Hebraism, the city also served as a significant site for the political awakening of Eastern European Jewry. In 1902 shoemaker Hirsh Lekert became a local revolutionary martyr and folk hero after he was sentenced to death for his assassination attempt on the local tsarist governor. By the twentieth century Jewish Vilna's communal libraries, schools, self-help organizations, and press contributed to the city's dynamic cultural landscape, providing locals with substantive local pride. If Warsaw had a demographic advantage and Łódź industrial ingenuity, Vilna had cultural leadership. By the 1920s the city asserted itself as the unofficial cultural capital of a transnational Yiddish-speaking homeland. Since no national community could claim majority status in Vilna, Yiddish played a prominent public role in the city's multicultural life and was promoted as a symbol of the national distinctiveness of Polish Jewry. Its Yiddish-speaking schools (including a gymnasium), teacher-training college, technical academy, athletic clubs, scouts, choir, theater groups, and five daily newspapers provided a way for the city's Jewish intelligentsia to rally Jews around Yiddish as a symbol of both civic and national solidarity. Yiddish was actively promoted as a component of *doikayt* (literarily, an ideological commitment to "hereness" that relied on Polish Jewry's sense of its cultural rootedness). When YIVO, the Jewish Scientific Institute, established itself in Vilna in 1925, the city could boast of hosting the leading Yiddish institution for advanced academic research in all of Poland, with projects focused on the history, folklore, philology, economics, demography, psychology, and education of Eastern European Jewry. Its expert scholars added to the city's sense of itself as a generator and exporter of ideas that drew inspiration from roots in a broad communal foundation.

It was in this environment that Sutzkever suddenly found himself as a young teenager. His mother settled the children in the working class Jewish neighborhood of Shnipeshik, across the river from both the traditional Jewish quarter with its narrow alleyways, arches, traditional study houses, and main synagogue complex, and the newer neighborhood of Pohulanka where many of the community's modern institutions and worldly intellectuals settled. The sudden death of his sister and his brother's decision to study in Paris and then emigrate to the Land of Israel left Sutzkever alone with just his mother. The family apartment overlooked an apple orchard, providing him with ample opportunity to gaze out at nature while recognizing in his mother's struggles the dignity of a life organized around cultural pride rather than material riches. Their neighborhood would go on to give birth to an impressive number of fellow Yiddish poets and artists who came of age as writers alongside Sutzkever in the 1930s.

Sutzkever himself did not benefit from a formal Yiddish education despite growing up in this center of modern Yiddish culture. His mother sent him to the local Talmud Torah, which provided scholarships for children in need, and then to a Polish-Hebrew high school. His initial experiments as a poet were in Hebrew, not Yiddish. Only later did he immerse himself in the classical and contemporary library of Yiddish literature through a disciplined program of self-study at the long reading table of the city's famed Strashun library and in the collection of the secular Yiddish Central Education Committee. Deep friendships with local scholars and writers also influenced his literary education. Dr. Max Weinreich was a critical early influence. Weinreich took time away from his work as director of YIVO to model engaged cultural activism, serving as the head scout for *Bin* (The Bee), the local Yiddishist scouting organization into which Sutzkever had been recruited. Sutzkever's scouting years encouraged an intimate bond with the natural beauty of the Lithuanian countryside through weekend hikes and summer camping retreats that would prove deeply influential for his poetry of the late 1930s. Weinreich, who had Sutzkever swear an oath of service to Yiddish culture as part of his induction into the scouts, later took him on as a YIVO fellow with whom he studied premodern Yiddish literature, providing the young writer with a sense of the classical roots of Ashkenaz (Zelig Kalmanovitsh and Noyekh Prilutski, YIVO's other prominent scholars of Yiddish literary history and linguistics, were also influential in this regard). Sutzkever's future wife Freydke Levitan, who worked as a bibliographer at YIVO and could recite Yiddish verse to him by heart, encouraged his literary ambitions at the same time that she won his heart. His general literary education was rounded out by discussions of Russian romanticism and symbolism (and even an introduction to Edgar Allen Poe) in the apartment and summer home of his friend Mikhl Tshernikhov (Astour), whose father was a local intellectual and Yiddish political activist associated with Territorialism, a movement that sought to secure Jewish cultural autonomy in hospitable lands. The courses on Polish literature that Sutzkever audited with Professor Manfred Kridl at the city's Stefan Batory University allowed him to adopt the Polish romantics as an equally important crosscultural literary influence.

Sutzkever's professional entrée into contemporary Yiddish poetry is associated with his inclusion in the literary and artistic group Yung-Vilne (Young Vilna), the last of the major modernist Yiddish groups in interwar Poland. Yung-Vilne did not have an official ideological or aesthetic program to which members were obliged, allowing it to attract a diverse group of ambitious talents who all excelled in their own genre. It included the poet Chaim Grade (who would go on to renown as the greatest prose writer to capture the traditional world of Lithuanian Jewry as it confronted the forces of modernity), the parodist Leyzer Volf, the fabulist Perets Miranski, the symbolist Elkhonen Vogler, the proletarian poets Shmerke Kaczerginski and Shimshn Kahan, the short story writer Moyshe Levin, and the artists Bentsie Mikhtom and Rokhl Sutzkever. They all integrated local concerns and settings into their work while keeping an eye on broader trends in contemporary Yiddish literature. In Yung-Vilne Sutkzever found a helpful combination of camaraderie and competition. His early poetry so resisted the leftist engagement expected of its membership that he was initially rejected by the group. Eventually, his publication elsewhere forced its members to take notice, and he was accepted into its fellowship. In "May Rains" (1934), one of his earliest published lyrics, Sutzkever identifies his immersion in nature as the primal source of poetry: "I burst out free and uncontrollably / into shimmering distances. / And I sing a hymn / to the life that dawns!" The poem frees the reader from the month of May's hackneyed proletarian associations to claim spring bloom as metaphor for poetic birth. Its speaker's disorientation gradually gives way to modernist liberation, as he suddenly finds himself *hefkerdik* (unclaimed) in nature, bursting free from all civilizing expectations in order to compose a psalm to existence outside the strictures of traditional liturgy. Similarly, when Sutzkever introduced himself to an overseas audience in the New York journal *Inzikh* with the lines "*Ot bin ikh dokh*— Here I Am, blooming as big as I am, / stung with songs as with fiery bees"—he was counting on the contrast between his earthy Yiddish and the familiar resonance of his ancient forefathers' Hebrew *hineni* ("Here I Am") to establish his work as a fresh, contemporary idiom for revelation.

Sutzkever went on to become one of Yung-Vilne's most productive members and enthusiastic organizers, bringing attention to its work through the prestige of his frequent publication in the leading Yiddish journals of New York and his riveting presence at local readings. He continued to represent the aesthetic, experimental wing of the group, who were in competition with its populists, debuting in the group's little magazine in 1935 with the provocation that "The sun is my flag and words are my anchor." Though Yung-Vilne would remain his creative home through his internment in the Vilna ghetto (where he organized an evening of readings in honor of its members as a way to raise communal spirits) in many ways he also was its anomaly. His thematic fascination with nature, faith in Yiddish poetry as a contemporary form of metaphysical exploration, and resistance to politics were out of step with the mood and expectations of Yiddish poetry in the mid-to-late 1930s, prompting literary critic Shmuel Niger to note that "Sutzkever sings solo." Sutzkever intuitively recognized this by reaching out to Arn-Glants Leyeles, one of the leading American Yiddish modernists and founders of Inzikh, whom he saw as a writer who shared his belief that poetry diminishes itself when it serves any cause other than itself.

Sutzkever's ambitious sequence "Shtern in shney" ("Stars in Snow," 1935) is an early case in point. It allowed him to challenge expectations of poetry set in Siberia, so often associated with exile and bleakness, while simultaneously showing off his neo-classical mastery over form and modernist interest in developing a metaphorical landscape for his emergence as a poet. Sutzkever divided the cycle into thirty-six sonnets, representing twice the numerical value of the Hebrew word for "life." At its center was a half-sonnet that marked the dividing line between childhood innocence and the transition to adult awareness. Throughout, Sutzkever reveled in new word combinations (*fliferd*—flying-horse, *vundervelder*—wonderwoods, *funkenshney*—sparklesnow, and *klangfiber*—soundfever) that yoked together the language of childhood discovery and poetic experience. The cycle's feast of light, color, and sound provides not only a distinctive visual and aural panorama but evokes the speaker's exuberant inner mood. In Sutzkever's hands, Siberia is transformed into a mythopoetic landscape of creative genesis, a world of endless wonder frozen in childhood memory and here translated into sound and color: "On the diamond blue snow / I write with the wind as with a pen, / drifting in the sparkling depths / of its childhood. I have never seen / such clearness that can overcome / all the lonely shadows of thought" ("Like a Sleigh in Its Wistful Ringing"). The beings with whom he communes—for instance, the snowman and the North Star—point to a moment before the vision of a child can distinguish between dream and reality, and before the soul of a poet is fully claimed by civilization. "Every summer, a fire snows on me, / every winter, glinting, you kling-klang in me. / May unceasing memory / be drawn to your blue smile. / May its sounds, claim, / remain over me my monument" ("North Star"). Though the cycle incorporates a father's death at its narrative center, the material struggles experienced by Sutzkever's biographical self are elided in favor of a subjective formulation of his birth as a writer. In the speaker's relationship with Tshanguri, a native Kirgiz boy that Sutzkever befriended in Omsk, Sutzkever allows Yiddish to experience a mystical exoticism that is at one with the universe. With his green eyes, furry pelt, pet camel, and flute, Tshanguri and the poet-speaker take off for adventures so far away from the family home that it is but a tiny dot on the horizon. Resting under the stars, the self-restraint of Jewish civilization left behind, the friends "kiss each blade of grass and leaf" as if it were a lover. Tshanguri was as important a poetic influence on young Sutzkever as were his scholarly and literary mentors in Vilna. The boys' friendship taught Sutzkever how to engage the natural world as mystical nourishment for his words. In a poem composed after the completion of the "Shtern in shney" cycle he reflects on the difference between a childhood in supposed exile in Siberia and the fully realized Jewish world in which he was composing his poetry in Vilna, complicating assumptions about Jewish home and homelessness: "I once had a homeland of clarity / (not like now, but a real one, a true one) / where dew kissed the cherry trees / in the freshness of a sun-drenched orchard . . . / There I had my own private heavens / and stars; an alef, a beys, and a gimel / through which I read golden poems / in the turquoise blue nights. / The sky has since clouded. / Its wisdom consists of blood. / My alphabet torn apart by the winds. / And it has been quite some time since I read poems / in the turquoise blue night."

Though Sutzkever initially wanted to publish "Shtern in shney" as its own volume, ultimately it was included as the final section of *Lider* (*Poems*, 1937), his first published collection of poetry. He then reworked the cycle during and after the war before its publication as *Sibir* (*Siberia*, 1952), the version upon which the translations included in this volume are based.

In *Lider* Sutzkever showed off his intimate sense of fellowship with the natural rhythms of the environments that gave birth to him as a writer. The volume was divided into four sections, one for each of the seasons, and was subdivided into fifty-two poems, one for each week of the year. Its mood stood in deliberate contrast to the anxiety of his local readers who were confronting rising Polish nationalism and worrisome threats from Nazi Germany. Instead, *Lider* offered up a way to read oneself as an organic part of a spiritual whole, to seek out a way for Yiddish poetry to serve as a new psalter for a life led outside the contours of formal religion. For instance, in "Blond Dawn" the distinction between sacred and profane time is collapsed when the daily sunrise is experienced as a *yontev* (a holiday). Even when Sutzkever turned his attention to social themes, rarely did his verse give in to gloominess or self-doubt. His natural predilection was for celebration, as when he described a march of Jewish youth as "a rivulet of sound" driving out the shadows "like bridges of light" ("Gates of the Ghetto"). What others would have read as political activism Sutzkever transforms into a release of sound, light, and primal energy. In its conflation of the self with nature, and poetry with the unending seasonal cycle of creative regeneration, *Lider* staked out a claim for the nourishing powers of Yiddish poetry to transcend the immediacy of the political moment.

One of the centerpieces of his first volume of poetry was an eight-part ballad about Cyprian Norwid, the only sketch of any writer to be included in his debut collection. Though Adam Mickiewicz (born in a town near Vilna) was the best-known Polish romantic in Jewish intellectual circles, Sutzkever was drawn to the inherent challenge of Norwid's verse and to his innovative use of archaisms that made room for neologisms and previously unexplored rhythmic possibilities. Of the dozens of poems dedicated to Norwid during the interwar burst of interest in the romantic writer among Polish modernists, Sutzkever's *Yiddish* ballad was the most monumental. It strategically anchored the section "Farb un klang" ("Color and Sound") devoted to exploration of the most elemental aspects of poetry. By holding up Norwid as a literary model above all other poets, Sutzkever claimed the entirety of the Polish literary tradition as his birthright. In the last years of the decade he published his own Yiddish translations of Polish poetry in the Vilna and Warsaw press in order to highlight kinships between two national literatures that shared the same borders.

Following the publication of *Lider* Sutzkever sought new ways to combine commitments to his art with his mounting public reputation. When anti-Jewish hooligans in the streets of Vilna attacked him in 1938, he responded by immersing himself even deeper in service to local Yiddish culture. He regularly mentored the next generation of aspiring writers in the newly formed group Yung-vald (Young Forest) and helped organize summer camps for the youth wing of the Yiddish Freeland movement. On the artistic side he took to excavating the premodern history of Yiddish literature as a way to draw inspiration for his work from classical sources. His intensive research with Max Weinreich at YIVO led to the publication of several experimental poems written in the Old Yiddish style. He also began work on a modern translation of Elia Bokher's early sixteenth century *Bove-bukh*, the most popular premodern Yiddish knightly romance.

Despite the storm clouds hanging over Europe, Sutzkever's poetic output in the years 1937–1939 showed a deepening faith in Yiddish poetry as a sacred realm. *Valdiks* (*Forested*), his second volume, appeared in 1940 when much of Polish Jewry was already under Nazi occupation and Vilna passed from Red Army occupation to Lithuanian rule. Given the context of its publication, its spiritual exuberance still surprises, as when he writes, "In everything I come upon I see a splinter of infinity," or, "Every moment without a hymn is a shame to me." Such lines were a statement of spiritual defiance, an affirmation of his claim over the Polish-Lithuanian landscape at a moment when Jews were regarded as alien, and an embrace of love over the paralyzing forces of fear or hatred. In the volume's confident sense of the self reflected in every manifestation of nature ("I see my body in the white of the birch tree / I feel my blood in the blooming of a rose") Sutzkever brings a neopantheistic streak into Yiddish poetry. Many of its poems follow the pilgrimage of an enigmatic forest-man as he communes with the "green temple" of nature in what Sutzkever refers to as *valdantplek* (forestrevelation): "The green doors open. / Eternal life, guide me to the mirror of my spirit." If white was the symbol of Sutzkever's Siberian genesis, like a blank page onto which childhood memories are carefully frozen in place, green emerges here as the signature hue to which Sutzkever would return for the remainder of his career. It was shorthand for the ways in which he saw his writing as an expression of a fundamental life impulse that transcended the profane challenge of time and proclaimed the sacredness of existence. Indeed, the final section of *Valdiks*, titled "Ecstasies," may be the most joyful release of poetic enthusiasm in all of Yiddish literature. To the cosmic muse he provides his poetic offering: "Now take up my word and my metaphor / And wherever you command, I will go." In later years Sutzkever observed that he cherished this volume more than any others. In it readers would find the definitive statement of his aesthetic worldview: "I am youth, I am beginning. . . . / Tell me: Why do people put up barriers / when I give myself to / joy, to driving away / sadness? / People believe that my bright light / distorts perspective, / but in the end I am rhythm / soul, music . . ."

Even before the Nazis arrived, Stalin's commissars returned to Vilna and seized it from the Lithuanian authorities. Sutzkever feared that his prewar affiliations and political unreliability as an aesthete might make him a target. He had written earlier to his brother in Palestine in an attempt to escape, but British limitations on Jewish immigration sealed his fate in Europe. Sutzkever and his wife Freydke attempted to outrun the German invasion in late June 1941 by fleeing east, but when the route became too precarious they turned back. During the roundup of local Jews in the initial weeks of Nazi occupation Sutzkever hid beneath the roof of his mother's house, pecking a hole in it to allow in just enough light to write. When, a short time later, he concealed himself in an empty coffin to evade the Germans, he resolved that no matter what "my word keeps on singing" ("I Lie in a Coffin"). A local peasant woman whom he would refer to later as "my rescuer" then took him in. Years later, he would write about a return back to Vilna where he would, thanks to her, come face to face with "my own double," pledging "I will tell it to my pencil." Those who had taken Sutzkever to task for his aesthetic aloofness before the war soon discovered that his belief in poetry as a transcendent domain only deepened the authority of his voice.

Sutzkever's two years in the Vilna ghetto reveal the full scope of his responsibility as a writer and as witness to the destruction of his community. During this period his artistic discipline and endurance were tested in unprecedented ways.

Within half a year of the German arrival more than two thirds of the city's Jews were killed. Most were shot in huge pits in the Ponary forest, a few kilometers from the city center. Sutzkever's own mother was betrayed and dragged from their apartment, never to be seen again. His guilt over his inability to protect her might have consumed him had he not worked through his own mourning poetically to hear her voice revive him: "So long as you are still here, then I exist too . . ." ("My Mother," 1942). After the period of mass slaughter Sutzkever and his wife found themselves confined to the ghetto. Most of his colleagues from Yung-Vilne were no longer around, either murdered at Ponary or refugees in the Soviet interior. He and Yung-Vilne colleague Kaczerginski joined the ghetto underground, the United Partisan Organization (FPO). Sutzkever devoted himself to the role of cultural organizer as a way to boost morale. He coordinated lectures, theater performances, and poetry readings. He was assigned to a work group of other intellectuals and writers whose task was to sort through the vast bibliographic and archival holdings the Nazis had gathered from dozens of local and regional libraries. Their work was part of a Nazi taskforce that wanted to loot the most valuable items to display after the German victory. The mass of books and documents Sutzkever and company were tasked with sorting was a repository of Jewish history, attesting to a religious and cultural heritage that extended back centuries. Every day Sutzkever would leave the ghetto gates for the former headquarters of the YIVO Institute, where some of the materials had been dumped. During long days of work, his comrades often allowed him moments of solitude from the sorting so that he could continue his writing. Even in wartime, the work of a poet was respected as a form of communal service. Instead of following orders, Sutzkever joined the secret activities of the Paper Brigade who took to hiding from Nazi hands and the paper mills the most priceless manuscripts and books by smuggling them back into the ghetto or to non-Jewish sympathizers for safekeeping. Their activities would have been a capital offense had they been discovered. Some of the group's rescued materials, which also included Sutzkever's own writings, were buried and retrieved after the war.

Sutzkever's poetic output during the war included meta-poetic meditations about the role of poetry in extremis, confessional lyrics about private losses and humiliations, and poems attesting to the stamina of the ghetto's teachers, cultural activists, and partisan fighters. His most famous poems of this period—"Teacher Mira," "The Lead Plates of the Rom Press," "A Wagon of Shoes," "To My Child," "Under Your White Stars," "Farewell"—are core works in the canon of Holocaust poetry. His lyrics were inspired by reality but not beholden to it, oftentimes groping toward the mythologizing needs of the moment. Sutzkever experimented with several longer works that reached toward the epic. "The Grave Child," inspired by the murder of his infant son in the ghetto hospital, has a solitary survivor of the killing at Ponary witness the birth of a Jewish child in a cemetery. Its haunting cry "The child must live!" helped earn Sutzkever first prize in the ghetto writers' competition in 1942. In "Kol Nidrei" the poet usurped the textual traditions of the high holiday liturgy and Hebrew prophets to compose a counter commentary on the fate of Eastern European Jewry. When "Kol Nidrei" was smuggled out of the ghetto to the Soviet Union, Ilya Ehrenburg published a Russian translation in *Pravda* that became one of the earliest accounts of the destruction of European Jewry to appear in the Soviet press. Despite the pressures of the moment his verse retained its prewar commitment to poetic precision by building on his preexisting belief in art as a counterforce to the powers of destruction. Several decades later, in the preface to an anthology of his wartime writings, he observed: "When the sun itself was transformed to ash I believed with full confidence that so long as poetry did not abandon me the bullet would not penetrate me." Though Sutzkever's achievement as a leading Yiddish poet of the Holocaust is not the focus of this volume of translations, it is nonetheless important to read Fein's selections with an awareness that everything the poet writes afterward is inflected by the tension between loss and regeneration.

Days before the final liquidation of the Vilna ghetto in September 1943, Sutzkever and Freydke escaped as part of a group of underground fighters. In the Narocz forests they joined up with a Soviet partisan unit. For the next six months, through a harsh winter, Sutzkever continued to write poetry and record the unit's activities while evading Nazi forces and their local collaborators. When the Jewish Anti-Fascist Committee in Moscow was alerted to the fact that Sutzkever was still alive, a rescue mission was put in place to retrieve him. His reputation made him a valuable witness to Jewish sacrifice in the struggle against fascism. Once in Moscow with Freydke, Sutzkever sought out friendships with fellow Yiddish and Russian-Jewish writers, several of whom would be purged by Stalin just a few years later. His articles in the Soviet press and radio broadcasts about the fate of Vilna's Jews, and Ilya Ehrenburg's article about him in *Pravda* in April 1944 transformed him into one of the first public figures to provide an eyewitness account to the destruction of European Jewry, prompting readers and listeners to share their own stories with him as part of an early process of testimonial exchange. Fate would have it that the poet initially rejected from Yung-Vilne for his exoticism and neoromanticism was now looked to as representative of an entire people.

Sutzkever's two years in Moscow were remarkably productive. He completed a Yiddish prose memoir of the ghetto (*From the Vilna Ghetto*), collected his wartime writings into two volumes (*The Fortress* and *Poems from the Ghetto*), and joined a committee of the Jewish Anti-Fascist Committee to gather materials for *The Black Book*, a testimonial history of the destruction of European Jewry that was later censored by the Soviet regime. Upon Vilna's liberation in spring 1944, he returned home for a period where he met up again with Kaczerginski and Abba Kovner, a Hebrew poet and Zionist leader of the ghetto underground. They retrieved materials secretly buried in the ghetto and set up a Jewish museum in Sutzkever's apartment. Their distrust of the Soviet regime led to the decision to secretly ferry the recovered materials to YIVO's headquarters, now in New York, where it remains as the Sutzkever-Kaczerginski archive. Sutzkever was later tasked in February 1946 with testifying on behalf of Soviet Jewry at the Nuremberg Trials.

Despite his welcome in Moscow, Sutzkever's longstanding wariness about communism persuaded him that one does not escape one totalitarian regime to establish oneself in another. Along with their infant daughter Reyne, the Sutzkevers were repatriated as Polish citizens to Łódź, and then moved on to Paris where he joined with a group of Yiddish refugee writers on the Seine and deepened his engagement with French symbolist poetry. It was during this period that he completed his first epic poem, *Geheymshtot* (*Secret City*), about a symbolic community of Jews who survive the liquidation of the ghetto in Vilna's sewers. The book-length work composed entirely in amphibrach tetrameter showcased Sutzkever's use of tight poetic form to construct a statement of restorative balance. At the same time, in immediate postwar collections such as *Yidishe gas* (*Jewish Street*) he grappled with the full specter of loss. In one of its feature poems, the ode "To Poland," Sutzkever made extensive use of citation from Polish poetry in order to convey the profundity of historical rupture and betrayal. With his prewar belief in the possibility of a Polish-Jewish cultural symbiosis now in tatters, its speaker struggles through the immensity of the task of bidding farewell: "How shall I raise a monument to the emptiness here? / How shall I reveal / for my grandchild's grandchild all our yesterdays / tomorrow?"

Of course, Sutzkever already had an answer. He boarded the immigrant ship *Patria*, arriving in Palestine in late 1947 in time to witness the reestablishment of Jewish sovereignty in the Land of Israel. Since Sutzkever had attended a Hebrew-speaking school as a child and had a brother in Palestine he did not harbor the same antipathies toward Zionism as did ideological Yiddishists. His reading of Jewish literature was sophisticated enough to appreciate that Hebrew and Yiddish were not competitors but complementary means of expression drawn from the same source. His experience with Zionist activists and poets in the ghetto furthered his belief that after the destruction of Polish Jewry the place for a Yiddish poet was among fellow Jews. Sutzkever was not unaware of the struggle that Yiddish speakers and writers faced in a new state ideologically committed to Hebrew, but he refused to engage in the language wars that had previously divided Eastern European Jews. "If the destruction was sung about in Yiddish," he insisted, "so too must the revival." Yiddish here plays an integrative role in holding the diverse chapters of his biography and Jewish culture together. Sutzkever could be both a proud Israeli and a Yiddish poet of the world.

In 1949, Sutzkever's reputation as a partisan poet convinced one of the institutional bastions of Zionism, its Hebrew labor union the Histadrut, to support the creation of a new Yiddish journal for which he would serve as editor. Sutzkever chose as its name *Di goldene keyt* (*The Golden Chain*), symbolizing a bond of culture between generations. Its title pointed back to an early twentieth century drama by Y. L. Peretz, who was regarded as one of the three classic writers to give birth to modern Yiddish literature. Peretz's spiritual drama spoke about the challenge of a time "between death and life, when the world hangs in doubt." It provided a vision of a Jewry with a sense of its own dignity, of "Sabbath and festival Jews" whose members danced and sang "with souls aflame." Words from the drama were engraved on Peretz's tomb in Warsaw, and it was this symbolic marker of Polish Jewry that Sutzkever imagined carrying on his back with him to the Land of Israel at the end of his ode "To Poland." Sutzkever insisted that his new journal, which borrowed its name from Peretz's drama, set the standard for postwar Yiddish scholarship and cultural discourse. For forty-six years it was the local address for Yiddish high culture, establishing Tel Aviv as one of the main centers of a postwar global Yiddish literary network. Since Sutzkever remembered well how important the literary fellowship of Yung-Vilne had been to him as a young writer, he was also an inspiration in the 1950s to the short-lived writers group Yung-Yisroel (Young Israel), which sought to encourage new Yiddish creativity in Israel.

Sutzkever encountered new Israeli landscapes with the same enthusiasm with which he had transformed his childhood in Siberia and the Lithuanian forests of young adulthood into mythopoetic landscapes of wonder and discovery. In *In fayervogn* (*In the Chariot of Fire*, 1952), his first volume of poems composed in Israel, he reveled in his new home's biblical terrains, pioneering agricultural communities, and ancient cities, just as he embraced the ingathering of Jews from far flung corners of the world. From its deserts where "Genesis exhibits its art" to Jerusalem's paranormal "mirror of stones" where one can "encounter eternity face to face and maybe not die," he saw Israel as a dynamic land of ingathering whose very existence was an occasion for poetry. Indeed, the opening section of the volume is titled "Shekheyonu," the traditional prayer of thanks-giving for the moment. At the same time, Sutzkever was under no illusion about the pressures on Yiddish in a young country where Hebrew was regarded as the ideological cornerstone for negation of diaspora, and the Holocaust was taboo as a subject in public culture: "We must not assimilate into Israel, we must assimilate Israel into ourselves." Sutzkever took to balancing his wonderment at the building of Jewish life in Israel with a respon-sibility toward the memory of Polish Jewry. He saw this as a nec-essary tension that would enrich and keep both in appropriate perspective. "It is a great privilege for a poet from the Jerusalem of Lithuania [Vilna] to have the Jerusalem of eternity take up his song . . . Now in Jerusalem I dream of Vilna as when I was in Vilna I dreamt of Jerusalem."

As witness to both the War of Independence (1948) and the Sinai Campaign (1956) Sutzkever saw continuity between his partisan comrades in Vilna and the spirit driving Israel's young combatants. After the fall of Jerusalem's Jewish quarter during the War of Independence he described his creative work in historical terms: "I saw how the Jews of Jerusalem erected ladders on rooftops in order to see the Western Wall. We writers must construct such ladders in poetry, so that [our readers] can observe the entirety of the Jewish world." The short volume *In midber Sinay* (*Sinai Desert*, 1957) is not only a Yiddish inter-vention into the tradition of Israeli war poetry, but it also tran-scends the immediate events on the battlefield to seek out the meaning of the Jewish return to Sinai, the very terrain that first forged their religious and national consciousness. In its desert wilderness Sutzkever's speaker communicated "a moment trans-parent to all time," a kind of transcendent revelation similar to those encountered during his earlier immersions in Siberia and the green forests of Lithuanian. In *Oazis* (*Oasis*, 1957–1959) he continued to explore how Israel spoke to and through him on the highest spiritual levels, as when he confesses in one lyric that "[t]here is a language here that does not require lips." *Gaystike erd* (*Spiritual Soil*, 1961), Sutzkever's second book-length epic, would be the apotheosis of what might be called his Yiddish-Zionist engagement. Returning to the period of his own immigration his poem is structured as a travelogue through the chaotic history of the years surrounding the birth of the Israeli state. Much like the ten representative Jews hiding in Vilna's sewers in his Holocaust epic *Secret City*, the speaker here gives voice to the varied experiences of newly arriving refugees, each a witness to private horrors. When the speaker gazes overboard from the rickety ship carrying them to the Land of Israel he sees a vision of his hometown swimming alongside it as a partner in their rebirth. Each of the poem's sections is devoted to a particular historical moment—the immigrant passage, the last days of the British Mandate, the Jewish underground struggle, the United Nations partition plan, the War of Independence. However, it is in its more intimate moments that the poem realizes the full scope of its ambition, as when he observes how the meaning of his daughter's Yiddish birth name Reyne (purity) is deepened by its slight shift into Hebrew as Rina (song of joy). The poem's epilogue is set on the ruins of Masada, one of the most popular Zionist pilgrimage sites, where the Jewish past was reinterpreted for contemporary ideological purposes. There, the speaker's youth as a partisan fighter back in Poland and his Israeli present merge as he gazes out from atop the Judean desert fortress on the anniversary of the Warsaw ghetto uprising. His presence is designed to emphasize a chain of self-sacrifice that runs through Jewish history that has contributed to this moment. As the white clouds carrying spring rains float past the sky-blue of the heavens and the Dead Sea below, the volume ends with a vision of the colors of Israel's flag, reading personal and political redemption onto the order of nature itself.

Beginning in the 1950s Sutzkever became a speaker in significant demand on the international Yiddish lecture circuit. His dramatic declamation in the tradition of great Russian poetry riveted audiences who were thirsty for a living link to a lost Atlantis. But as the speaker in one of his poems reminds him: "And if you paint over the image of the Yiddish street / with a brush dipped in your sunny palette / Know this: the fresh colors will peel / and someday the old colors will attack you with an axe. . . ." Sutzkever's personal aesthetic challenge, then, was to balance the collective need for a language of memorialization with his natural disposition toward a modernist, affirmative language of existential communion. The two came together in his most stylistically ambitious volume of the decade, *Ode tsu der toyb* (*Ode to the Dove*, 1955). Its three sections synthesize and complement his various commitments, while allowing each a distinct realm. The opening section and title poem exhibited Sutzkever's neoclassical delight at working within boundaries of strict poetic form and exploring the meaning of living poetically. In its opening ode the speaker recalls his childhood rescue of a dove. The bird and child engage in a pact to ensure that the gift of the muse remains with him throughout his life: "So long as I inspire you / come whenever I call you, in rain and in snow and in fire." By contrast, the volume's middle section, inspired by a visit to Africa a few years earlier, performs primal, modernist release through the free-verse cycle "Elephants at Night." The volume's concluding, phantasmagoric section consisted of "Green Aquarium," experimental prose narratives set in the shell of the former ghetto where the narrator is confronted by lone survivors who come to him with their stories. Its metafictional considerations include the reminder to mind one's aesthetic choices as if one's life depends on it: "Stroll through words as you would walk through a minefield: one false step, one false move and the lifetime of words strung on your veins will be blown apart with you." Here, the green aquarium serves as a metaphor for the power of writing to provide eternal life, so long as one invests completely in the highest standards of artistry.

The 1960s were an important moment for Sutzkever to take stock of a career that had already spanned three decades and to turn his attention to the task of anthologizing. In rapid succession he published a two-volume edition of his collected poetry *Poetishe verk* (1963), divided chronologically and geographically between a volume of his European writings and another that begins with his arrival in Israel. Then he coedited the groundbreaking anthology of writings by Soviet-Yiddish writers *A shpigl af a shteyn* (*Mirror on a Stone*, 1964), which served as a testament to the culture decimated by Stalin. In 1968, Sutzkever compiled *Lider fun yam-hamoves* (*Songs from the Sea of Death*), an authoritative edition of his Holocaust writings. The following year he was the inaugural recipient of the Itsik Manger Prize for Yiddish. He would go on to win the Israel Prize, the country's highest cultural honor, in 1985.

The late 1960s inaugurate yet another stage in Sutzkever's writing. His poems take on a retrospective and more philosophical character, marked by deeper metaphysical and metapoetic musings, poems about other writers and artists, and ongoing experimentation with Yiddish versification. *Di fidlroyz* (*The Fiddle-Rose*, 1974) and *Lider fun togbukh* (*Diary Poems*, 1977) are astonishing statements of poetic self-confidence in an age that regarded the Yiddish poet as an anachronism. In *Tsviling-bruder* (*Twin Brother*, 1986), Sutzkever once again constructs a volume of thirty-six poems, the Hebrew numerical equivalent for double-life, as a distillation of his multiple twin selves—the autobiographical self and the poetic "I," the prewar and postwar self, child and adult perspectives—which he puts into conversation by circling back to and expanding on some of his most intimate early symbology. In these later works, his father's fiddle, the snowman and North Star from his prewar *Siberia* cycle, and Edenic greens reappear, though not primarily in the service of memory. Rather, Sutzkever establishes creation as the only convincing alternative to oblivion, poetic beauty as the antidote to the moral ugliness of history, striking a tone that resists cynicism in favor of communion. It is for this reason that some readers consider his work from this period akin to a contemporary Yiddish psalter, "writ[ten] with lightening on parchment clouds."

Fein borrows the title for this volume of translations—*The Full Pomegranate*—from a poem of this period. Long an ancient motif of fertility (and the title of one of the most visually stunning Yiddish periodicals in Weimar Berlin), in Sutzkever's hands "the full pomegranate" is a metonym for poetry, each of its genesis-seeds a unique expression of creative potential embedded in the red flesh of experience: "The pomegranate, full—youth is in its oldness, / oldness is in its youth. It holds both / inward in its full root cellar— / death and life unwilling to separate." The speaker's invitation to "live in my pomegranate arch, / radiant and sliced open" proposes life in poetry as a transcendent act.

When the speaker of one lyric from his diary poems asks the universal human question "Who will last, what will last?" the speaker responds by locating eternity in the most fleeting vestiges of nature—the ocean's foam, a cloud snagged in a tree, a single syllable, a drop of wine in a jug—only turning in the final lines to a Jewish rhetorical strategy by answering a big question with one of his own, unlikely to satisfy believers or skeptics alike: "Who will last, what will last? God will last. / Isn't that enough for you?" During this period Sutzkever also deepens the partnership between his personal ghosts and his own creativity, acknowledging them as beloved interlocutors in metaphysical discourse: "They [the dead] love to hear my poems, so I read to them. / I say: There is no death. Then I hear a protest: / Death is our life; is there, then, no longer life either?" ("Elegiacally," *From Old and Young Manuscripts*). Such musings prompt the ongoing development of his belief in eternity as the simultaneity of past, present, and future moments, as "time steal[ing] across borders" ("Twin-Brother"). His late poetry eschews cynicism or postmodern angst in favor of integrating the synchronic and diachronic strains of his mythopoetic worlds so that their intimate, national, and cosmic strands are realized as a unity: "All that is past, experienced, previous, / now floats through me and through my temples / like twilight clouds, in order / to re-live what was outlived, / and to see again what was seen" (["All that is past . . ."], 1996).

AS WE READ RICHARD FEIN'S FRESH TRANSLATIONS OF Sutzkever I return to what it has meant to me to be fortunate enough to have Yiddish poetry in my life. My twenties were marked by seminars (and long nights before open dictionaries) that revealed a library that at one point had provided a vocabulary of contemporary existence to Yiddish readers grappling with rapid geopolitical and cultural challenges. As I get older, my appreciation remains for the experimentalism of American Yiddish modernists. But their belief in Yiddish poetry as world poetry that could not only compete with the latest trends in modernist verse but even serve as its vanguard ultimately could not sustain a generation of readers beyond its own. Similarly, the abandon of revolutionary Yiddish poets such as Moyshe Kulbak ("*Hey, lomir geyen, lomir geyen! / lomir do iberlozn di shvakhe . . .*" [Hey, let us go, let us go! Let's leave the weak ones behind . . .]) and Perets

Markish ("*Mayn nomen iz: 'atsind'* ..." [My name is: "Now" ...]) continues to thrill, but the promise of their enthusiasm cannot be read without the knowledge that the very revolution that raised their hopes ultimately devoured them. Itsik Manger's radical rewriting of biblical lore remains the greatest accomplishment of poetic midrash, just as Rokhl Korn's "other side of the poem" and Kadya Molodowski's "paper bridge" are suggestive tropes for wrestling with Yiddish verse as the repository of cultural memory. Each of these Yiddish poets (and there are so many others!) became for their readers an interpretive window onto the world. Yet only Sutzkever provides a body of poetic writing that remains accessible even as it consistently renews itself, and in so doing renews its readers. No other poet maintains as deep a respect for the powers of Yiddish creativity to seek out beauty in chaos, and harmony from the bloody disharmonies of twentieth century Jewish experience. Quite simply, Sutzkever is the most spiritually nourishing poet in the Yiddish poetic canon.

It has already been a generation since Barbara and Benjamin Harshav's *A. Sutzkever: Selected Poetry and Prose* (1991) showcased Sutzkever's poetic and prose oeuvre in a single volume. Over the years English translations of discrete Sutzkever volumes have included *Siberia: A Poem* (trans. Jacob Sonntag, 1961), *Burnt Pearls: Ghetto Poems of Abraham Sutzkever* (trans. Seymour Mayne, 1981), *In the Sinai Desert* (trans. David and Roslyn Hirsch, 1987), *The Fiddle Rose: Poems 1970–1972* (trans. Ruth Whitman, 1990), and *Laughter Beneath the Forest*: *Poems from Old and Recent Manuscripts* (trans. Barnett Zumoff, 1996). Sutzkever translations are featured in such classic anthologies as *The Golden Peacock* (1961), *The Penguin Book of Modern Yiddish Verse* (1987), and *An Anthology of Modern Yiddish Poetry* (1995). Ruth Wisse's translation of his prose masterpiece *Green Aquarium* in *Prooftexts* (1982) will be joined soon by my own translation of his memoir *Vilna Ghetto*. From translations of individual poems by established American poets such as Jacqueline Osherow to a new generation of Yiddish poet-translators such as Maia Evrona, Sutzkever remains one of the enduring representatives of Yiddish to world literature.

Richard Fein's *The Full Pomegranate* now joins Heather Valencia's *Still My Word Sings* (2017) in allowing us to encounter Sutzkever anew through a volume of carefully curated verse. Fein's selections eschew comprehensiveness in favor of reengaging Sutzkever as a writer who draws the reader back to the spiritual and aesthetic powers of the Yiddish poem itself, or as Sutzkever would have it, where one can ". . . see the eternal that remains outside of death; / I even have a name for it: radiant core." Fein accords the Yiddish poems full respect alongside his translations, allowing those with access to Yiddish the added interpretive pleasure of reading Sutzkever simultaneously between languages. He recognizes that translation is a strategic craft designed to serve both poet and reader, and he is faithful in his responsibilities to both.

Since Sutzkever's life was very much a life lived in and through poetry it is fitting that he is translated for us here by Richard Fein, a contemporary poet who has contributed to the cultural landscape of Yiddish in America for more than three decades, through his essays (*The Dance of Leah*, 1986, and *Yiddish Genesis*, 2012), translations (*Selected Poems of Yankev Glatshteyn*, 1989, and *With Everything We've Got: A Personal Anthology of Yiddish Poetry*, 2009), and an original lyric voice that is often in conversation with his most beloved Yiddish writers. Few contemporary American poets have sustained as substantive an engagement with Yiddish in their own writing as Richard Fein, and none has written as meaningfully about the ways in which his translations from it are "a dimension of himself." Fein's relationship with Yiddish is visceral, even preternatural. In his essays he acknowledges that "I often feel that Yiddish possesses me rather than the other way around. . . ." He has confessed the ways in which "[t]ranslation for me is a form of second birth," and how "the allure of Yiddish poetry . . . is not so much to translate it as to absorb it until it becomes part of my own poetry." I am moved by the ways in which he situates the source of his own poetry in the dialogic act of translating others. "It was through Yiddish—those sounds of my instinctual being I once fled—that I came back to the writing of poetry." Let us end, then, with Fein's own poetic voice. If the remainder of this volume is an exercise in his generosity—for what is the act of translating a fellow writer other than the gift of reincarnation?—we should take notice here of the intimacy of his profound relationship with Yiddish.

> You reach to me like a lover
> wanting one more kiss.
> How long it's taken for us to embrace,
> for our tongues to find each other.
> ("Yiddish")

I take Fein's image of tongues reaching out for one another as an invitation to think anew about the relationship between Yiddish and contemporary Jewish culture lived beyond Jewish languages. In Fein's imagination, they engage in the most passionate desire as lovers who seek out, and ultimately rely on, one another to realize their full meaning. Here, Fein grafts his own permanent link onto Sutzkever's golden chain, providing a new generation of readers with a definitive statement of why Yiddish, and Sutzkever, continue to matter.

SMITH COLLEGE (NORTHAMPTON, MA) AND TEL AVIV
JULY 2018

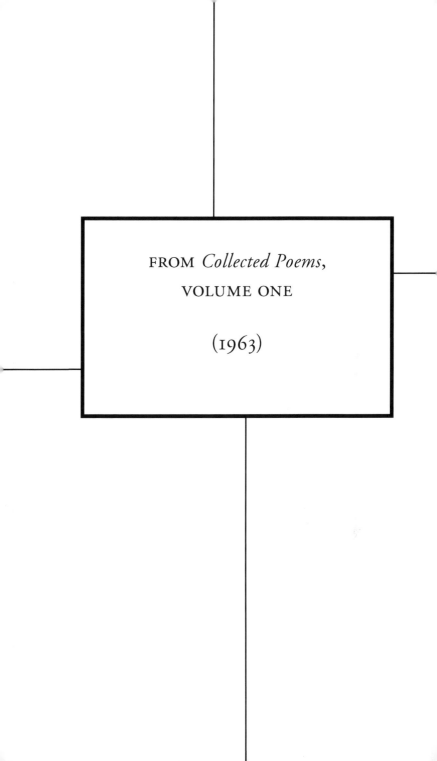

FROM *Collected Poems*,
VOLUME ONE

(1963)

Siberia

IN THE VILLAGE

I

Sunset on icy blue paths.
Sweet dozing colors in my soul.
A little house shines across from the valley
covered with the snow of sunset.
Wonderwoods swaying on windowpanes,
magic sleighs chiming in a circle.
Cooing of doves in the little attic,
cooing at my face. Under ice,
striped through with dazzling crystals,
the Irtysh quivers, half real.
Under speechless domes
a world blooms—a child of seven years.

סיביר

אין כּוטער

א

זונפֿאַרגאַנג אויף אײזיק בלאָע װעגן.
זיסע דרעמלפֿאַרבן אין געמיט.
ס׳ליכט פֿון טאָל אַ שטיבעלע אַנטקעגן
מיט אַ שניי פֿון זונפֿאַרגאַנג באַשיט.
װוּנדערװעלדער הוידען זיך אויף שויבן,
צויבער־שליטנס קלינגען אין אַ קרײז.
אויפֿן פֿיצל בוידעם װאָרקען טויבן,
װאָרקען אויס מײן פּנים. אונטער אײז,
דורכגעשטרטימפֿט מיט בליציקע קרישטאָלן
צאָפֿלט דער אירטיש אין האַלבער װאָר.
אונטער אויסגעשװויגענע קופֿאָלן
בליט אַ װעלט—אַ קינד פֿון זיבן יאָר.

In the light-dark snowed-under
village of my childhood in Siberia
blossoms bloom from shadows' eyes—
countless quicksilver blossoms.
The moon flings its dazzle into
dimmed, extinguished corners.
My father—white as the moon,
the stillness of snow in his hands.
He slices the black bread with the gleaming
merciful knife. His face blues.
And with freshly cut thoughts
I dip my father's bread in the salt.

אינעם ליכטיק־טונקעלן, פֿאַרשנייטן
כוטער פֿון מײַן קינדהייט אין סיביר,
בליִען פֿון די שאַטן־אַפּלען—קווייטן,
קוועקזילבערנע קווייטן אָן אַ שיעור.
אין די ווינקלען אָפּגעלאָשן מאַטע
בלאָזט אַרײַן לבֿנה איר געבלענד.
ווײַס ווי די לבֿנה איז דער טאַטע,
שטילקייט פֿונעם שניי—אויף זײַנע הענט.
ער צעשנײַדט דאָס שוואַרצע ברויט מיט בלאַנקן
רחמימדיקן מעסער. ס׳פּנים בלויט.
און מיט נײַ צעשניטענע געדאַנקען
טונק איך אינעם זאַלץ דעם טאַטנס ברויט.

3

Knife. Father. Smoky kindling.
Childhood. Child. A shadow takes the violin
down from the wall. And thin-thin-thinner
snowsounds fall upon my head.
Quiet. It's father playing. And the sounds—
engraved in air, just as a silvery
blue breath in the frost suspended
over the moon-glazed snow.
Through a furry frieze of ice on the pane,
a wolf smells the flesh of music.
Quiet. In our dovecote a pigeon
pecks through an eggshell—peck-peck.

מעסער. טאַטע. רויכיקע לוטשינע.
קינדהייט. קינד. אַ שאָטן נעמט אַראָפּ
ס׳פֿידעלע פֿון וואַנט. און דין־דין־דינע
שנייענקלאַנגען פֿאַלן אויף מײַן קאָפּ.
שטיל. דאָס שפּילט דער טאַטע. און די קלאַנגען—
אויסגראַווירט אין לופֿטן, ווי אין פֿראָסט
זילבערלעך פֿון אָטעם בלאָ צעהאַנגען
איבער שנײַ לבֿנהדיק באַגלאָזט.
דורך אַן אײַזיק אָנגעפֿעלצטן שײַבל
שמעקט אַ וואָלף צום פֿלײַש פֿון דער מוזיק.
שטיל. אין אונדזער טויבנשלאַק אַ טײַבל
פּיקט זיך פֿון אַן אײַעלע, פּיק־פּיק.

AT DAWN

The marker-paws some animal
has sown like roses in the snow
were barely gilded from above
when the sun—unknown, new—
cast its spearlike cry.
Below still darkens. Forest roots
grind their teeth deep in the ground.
The dog, hitched to the sled,
vents living steam. The steam meets
glowing chimney smoke and
a human breath rising from the scene—
until a tent hangs in the air.

פֿאַר טאָג

די סימנים־לאַפּעס, וואָס אַ חיה
האָט פֿאַרזײט װי רױזן אינעם שניי,
װען די זון, אַן אומבאַקאַנטע, נײע,
האָט דערלאַנגט איר שפּיזיקן געשרײ—
זענען קוים באַגילדט פֿון אױבן. אונטן
פֿינצטערט נאָך. די װאָרצלען פֿונעם װאַלד
קריצן מיט די צײן אין טיפֿע גרונטן.
פֿונעם הונט, געשפּאַנט אין שליטן, פֿראַלט
לעבעדיקער דאַמף. דער דאַמף באַגעגנט
שטײגנדיק אַ קױמענרױך װאָס העלט
און אַ מענטשן־אָטעם פֿון דער געגנט—
ביז אין לופֿט בלײבט העַנגען אַ געצעלט.

9

RECOGNITION

I

"Oh, Father, tell me—where does the world end?!"
Philosophical, I demand a solution.
An answer comes: "Behind that hut
on the top of the mountain, where the sun sets."
Really? *Really?* So . . . without a second thought
I have to catch up to the sunset! And I run
upward through a silver net of tears to
where the world itself ends, up the mountain.
My eyes demand of the god of Siberia
not to let my longing be in vain.
All the years pre-me, aeons of them,
quiver in the snow: "Welcome."

דערקענטעניש

א

,,זאָג, ווו ענדיקט זיך די וועלט, אָ, טאַטע?!‟
פֿילאָסאָפֿיש מאָן איך אַ באַשייד.
קומט אַן ענטפֿער: ,,הינטער יענער קאַטע
אויפֿן באַרגשפּיץ, ווו די זון פֿאַרגייט‟.
אמת טאַקע ? אויב אַזוי,—ניט קלערן,
אַניאָגן די שקיעה! און איך לויף
אויבן, דורך אַ זילבערנעץ פֿון טרערן,
ווו די וועלט זיך ענדיקט, באַרג־אַרויף.
ביים סיבירער גאָט די אויגן מאָנען,
ס׳זאָל ניט זײַן מײַן בענקעניש אומזיסט.
אַלע יאָרן ביז־מיר, יאָר־מיליאָנען,
צאַפּלען פֿון די שנייען: זײ באַגריסט.

2

Behind me—a little dot of a father.
The sun facing me, my heart is racing.
Finally, I ran all the way up to the hut!
The tension lures me on, won't leave.
My lips are drawn to the bonfire
shedding light down to the howling bottom.
Daddy! The world stretches beyond,
without an end—none, none, none.
My father doesn't hear. Green stars fall.
My father doesn't see. And from out of nowhere
I a child turn into an avalanche
whom light and wonder shaped.

הינטער מיר—אַ פּינטעלע אַ טאַטע.

ס׳האַרץ, דער זון אַנטקעגן, אין גאַלאָפּ.

שוין, דערלאָפֿן אויבן צו דער קאַטע!

נאָר די שפּאַנונג מאַניעט, לאָזט ניט אָפּ.

מײַנע ליפֿן ציִען זיך צום שיטטער,

וואָס באַשײַנט דעם ווײַענדיקן דנאַ.

טאַטינקעו! עס ציט די וועלט זיך ווײַטער,

און קיין סוף—ניטאָ, ניטאָ, ניטאָ.

טאַטע הערט ניט. שטערן פֿאַלן גרינע.

טאַטע זעט ניט, אַז פֿון העלער הויט

ווער איך פֿון אַ ייִנגל—אַ לאַווינע,

וועמען ליכט און ווּנדער האָט געבוירט.

LIKE A SLEIGH IN ITS WISTFUL RINGING

On the diamond blue snow
I write with the wind as with a pen,
drifting in the sparkling depths
of its childhood. I have never seen
such clearness that can overcome
all the lonely shadows of thought.
Like a sleigh in its wistful ringing,
my life resounds thin and long
over the eveningsteppe, where
the moon lurks, cuddled in its mirror,
with its nose facedown,
and two wings spread out free.

ווי אַ שליטן אין פֿאַרבענקטן קלינגען

אויפֿן שניי דעם דימענטענעם, בלאָען
שרײַב איך מיטן ווינט ווי מיט אַ פּען,
בלאָנדזשע אויף די גלימערדיקע דנאָען
פֿון זײַן קינדהייט. האָב נאָך ניט געזען
אַזאַ לויטערקייט, וואָס קאָן באַצווינגען
אַלע עלנט־שאָטנס פֿון געדאַנק.
ווי אַ שליטן אין פֿאַרבענקטן קלינגען
גלעקלט דאָ מײַן לעבן דיר און לאַנג
דורכן אָוונטסטעפּ, וואָס אין זײַן שפּיגל,
צוגעטוליעט מיט דער נאָז אַראָפּ,
לויערט די לבֿנה, און צוויי פֿליגל
שלאָגן אָפּ.

FIERY PELT

Fields—gleaming, glowing metals;
Trees—molded in stone.
Snow has no place to fall;
the sun wears a fiery pelt.
With its diamond paintbrush
the artist Frost paints on my skull,
as on a windowpane, its colorful snow legends,
and "signs" with the flight of a dove.
The sun sets in me. The sun—no more.
Only its fiery pelt is seen
on a long branch. And I—speechless—
want to put it on before it dies away.

פֿײַערדיקער פֿעלץ

פֿעלדער—בלאַנקע, בלענדיקע מעטאַלן,
ביימער—אָפּגעגאָסענע מיט פֿעלדז.
שנײיען האָבן מער ניט וווּ צו פֿאַלן,
ס׳טראָגט די זון אַ פֿײַערדיקן פעלץ.
מיט זײַן דימענט־פֿענדזל אויף מײַן שאַרבן
מאָלט דער קינסטלער פֿראָסט ווי אויף אַ שויב
זײַנע שנײַי־לעגענדעס פֿול מיט פֿאַרבן,
,,שרײַבט זיך אונטער׳׳ מיט געפֿלי פֿון טויב.
זון פֿאַרגייט אין מיר. ניטאָ די זון מער.
בלויז מע זעט איר פֿײַערפֿעלץ אַליין
אויף אַ לאַנגער צוווײַג. און איך—אַ שטומער—
אָנטאָן וויל אים ערבֿ זײַן פֿאַרגיין.

IN A SIBERIAN FOREST

I

Young sun, perpetual new-born, → everyday sunrise
rolls around with me in the snow.
My father says, "My child, let's go
get some wood from the forest,"
and our silver colt is hitched to a sledge.
The axe gleams. The sharpened sunknives * oxymerons
cut up the day into snowflames.
Dustsparks—my breath! And a race   *cold morning
over the steppe of sleeping bears   breathing into
through sunwebs. The snow chimes in.   air
All the stars poured down last night   ↓
lie frozen now, at rest.   magical

* nature is kinetic

אין אַ סיבירער וואַלד

א

יונגע זון, וואָס אייביקט ניַי געבאָרן,
קיַיקלט זיך אין שניי מיט מיר ביַינאַנד.
זאָגט דער טאַטע: ,,קינד מיַינס, לאָמיר פֿאָרן
ברענגען האָלץ פֿון וואַלד׳׳. און ס׳ווערט געשפּאַנט
אונדזער זילבער־לאָשיק אין אַ שליטן.
ס׳בלאַנקט די האַק. אין פֿלאַמענשניַי דער טאָג
פֿון געשליַיפֿטע זונמעסערס צעשניטן.
פֿונקענשטויב—דער אָטעם! און אַ יאָג
איבער סטעפּ פֿון שלאָפֿנדיקע בערן
דורכן זונגעוועב. דער שניי קלינגט צו.
אַלע נעכטן אָפּגעשיטע שטערן
ליגן איצט פֿאַרפֿראָראָרענע, אין רו.

2

Forest. A fresh dazzle on the branches
exhales wolf howls.
Glowing echo of silence—
you shoot a hot arrow into me.
Each snowflake is a tiny frozen bell,
touch it and it answers with a ring,
and the ring—shatters into a thousand pieces.
Suddenly a little fox shows me his tongue
from his snowtent and slinks back in.
"Little fox, don't be afraid!"—And my cheek
warms itself from the suspended sparks,
until the sun sinks in my father's axe.

וואַלד. אַ פֿרישע בליציקייט אויף צוווייגן
אָטעמט אויס דעם וואַלדפֿישן געהיל.
אָנגעגליטער עכאַ פֿונעם שוווייגן—
שיסט אין מיר אַרײַן אַ הייסע פֿײַל.
יעדער שניי איז אַ פֿאַרפֿראָרן גלעקל,
גיב אַ ריר און ס׳ענטפֿערט מיט אַ קלונג,
און דער קלונג—אויף טויזנט אַ צעברעקל.
פֿלוצעם וויזט אַ פֿיקסל מיר די צונג
פֿונעם שנייגעצעעלט און שוין פֿאַרזונקען.
—,,פֿיקסל, האָב ניט מורא !''—און מײַן באַק
וואַרעמט זיך בײַ העננגענדיקע פֿונקען,
ביז די זון פֿאַרגייט אין טאָטנס האַק.

3

As we travel back to the quiet village—
my soul still strays in the forest.
And the calm, genial forest
warms and radiates my soul in its bosom.   *calming*
Stars start to crown me with song,   } *Being apart/connection*
stars kindled in the wind.
In reverence to stars, an urge to cry . . .
until the last tree in the forest disappears,
and the ruts stand still in the snow.
Then my father's voice wakens me.
I see: The moon is in the sledge,
accompanying me to my home in the valley.

ציִען מיר אַהײם צום שטילן כּוטער—
בלאָנדזשעט מיַין נשמה נאָך אין וואַלד.
און דער וואַלד אַ גוטער, אַ באַרוטער,
וואַרעמט זי אין בוזעם און באַשטראַלט.
נעמען שטערן מיט געזאַנג מיך קרייִנען,
שטערן אױפֿגעבלאָזענע אין ווינט!
און לכּבֿוד שטערן ווילט זיך וויינען . . .
ביז דער לעצטער בוים פֿון וואַלד פֿאַרשווינדט,
און עס בליַיבן שטײַען אין שניי די שניטן.
דעמאָלט וועקט מיך אױף דעם טאָטנס קול.
זע איך: די לבֿנה איז אין שליטן
מיטגעפֿאָרן צו מיַין הײם אין טאָל.

TO MY FATHER

Papa, I ran after the sledge
carrying your coffin, and held
a snow-white pigeon against my breast,
trying to catch up to your memory.
When the heartbeat of the pickaxe
hacked out your new hut, abyss
that swallowed you up where
you still glitter under the ice,
I wanted to fall in there with you!
But my pigeon suddenly flew off,
crested golden white by the evening sun,
and drew me back to life . . .

צום טאַטן

טאַטע, נאָכן שליטן מיט דײַן אָרון
נאָכגעלאָפֿן בין איך דיר, כּדי
אָנצוּיאָגן ערגעץ דײַן זכּרון
מיט אַ טויב אין בוזעם ווײַס ווי שניי.
ווען עס האָט אַ כוטער דיר אַ נײַעם
אויסגעהאַקט אַ האַרצקלאָפֿיקער לאָם,
און פֿאַרשלונגען האָט דיך באַלד אַ תּהום,
ווו די פֿינקלסט אונטער אײַז עד־היום—
האָב איך דאָרט אַרײַנפֿאַלן געוואָלט!
נאָר מײַן טויב איז דעמאָלט גראָד פֿאַרפֿלויגן,
אָוונטזון באַקרײַנט מיט ווײַסן גאָלד,
און אַרויף צום לעבן מיך געצויגן . . .

25

IRTYSH

Shh! Where's that sound coming from?
The Irtysh wants to flee from its bank!
It seeks in cold, wavy rings
ebbing faces of days.
It opens its eyes to the stars
from a carved-out circle: "How long
will the spring not hear my plea,
will my song not cut through the ice?"
Night hums a secret into its beard:
"A sun is already being forged!" and
straightaway, a star falls from a thread
and—a kiss on the wintry river.

אירטיש

שטיל! פֿון וואַנען קוואַלט אַזאַ מיין קלינגען?
ס׳וויל אַנטלויפֿן דער אירטיש פֿון ברעג!
זוכט אין קאַלטע, כוואַליעדיקע רינגען
אָפּגעפֿליגטע פֿנימער פֿון טעג.
עפֿנט ער די אויגן צו די שטערן
פֿון אַן אויסגעזעגגטן ראַד: ,,ווי לאַנג
וועט דער פֿרילינג מיין געבעט ניט הערן,
וועט דעם איז ניט שניידן מיין געזאַנג?‘‘
זשומעט נאָכט אין באַרד אַרײַן אַ סוד אים:
— ,,ס׳ווערט שוין אויסגעשמידט אַ זון!‘‘ און גלײַך
פֿאַלט אַראָפּ אַ שטערנדל פֿון פֿאָדעם
און— אַ קוש דעם ווינטערדיקן טײַך.

27

SNOWMAN

I

Snowman, monument of childhood, guardian
of a frozen treasure! It's not for nothing
I thoroughly believe: you are my commander.
Snowman, I hail you a thousand times!
You are the god of children and of winds,
and near you my dream stands kneeling.
"Snowman," whole families of wolves
come, crying out, "guard us, shield us!"
Snowman, you are eternal, your sparkle-armor
of crystal will never melt.
Snowman, how beautifully you dance on your stilts
for the little starmen in the valley!

שניימענטש

א

שניימענטש, דענקמאָל נאָך אַ קינדהייט, היטער
פֿון אַ קאַלטן אוצר! ניט אומזיסט
גלייבן גלייב איך: דו ביסט מײַן געביטער.
זײַ מיר, שניימענטש, טויזנט מאָל באַגריסט!
ביסט דער גאָט פֿון קינדער און פֿון ווינטן,
לעבן דיר מײַן חלום שטייט געקניט.
ס׳קומען וועלף אין גאַנצענע געזינטן
און זיי רופֿן: שניימענטש, היט, באַהיט!
אייביק ביסטו שניימענטש, ניט צעשמאָלצן
ווערט דײַן פֿינקל־פֿאַנצער פֿון קרישטאָל.
אָ, ווי שיין דו טאַנצסט אויף דײַנע שטאָלצן
פֿאַר די שטערנמענטשעלעך אין טאָל!

2

Snowman, oaf, with a pot on your head
instead of a crown!
Show once again your smile in the haze,
warm up my loneliness with your ice.
If my longing finally reaches you—
go in those very marks left by my feet,
and you will find me in a small
shul of sound praying to snow.
If you don't find me there, forgive me,
for clearly we have missed each other.
Inherit my former presence in that shul,
complete the breath of my time.

שנײַמענטש, אומגעלומפּער, מיט אַ טעפּל
אויפֿן קאָפּ אַנשטאַט אַ קרוין! באַװײַז
נאָך אַ מאָל דײַן שמײכל פֿונעם נעפּל,
װאַרעם אָן מײַן עלנט מיט דײַן אײַז.
אויב מײַן בענקשאַפֿט איז צו דיר דערגאַנגען—
אין די זעלבע טריט־סימנים גײ,
װעסטו אין אַ שטיבעלע פֿון קלאַנגען
מיך געפֿינען תּפֿילה טאָן צו שנײ.
ניט געפֿונען—האָב ניט קיין פֿאַראיבל,
קעגנטיק, אַז מיר האָבן זיך געמיִדט.
ירשן מײַן געװוינזנקייט פֿון שטיבל
און פֿאַרענדיק אָטעמען מײַן צײַט.

SIBERIAN SPRING

I

Multi-colored wings flap
in the wind over taiga-wilderness.
As if a mirror is melting, mile
after mile trickles and wells up,
edges greening. Wet snow sings farewell,
wings, mirrors full of color and sound.
With young lion-roars from rains
childhood desire flares up
to overtake all wild streams,
to take off like a bird
over people, forest, fields, chasms—
to the festive new day!

סיבירער פֿרײליגג

א

ס׳נעמען פֿאַטשן פֿילקאָלירטע פֿליגל
איבער טײגע־ווילדערניש אין ווינט.
ס׳קוואַלט און ריזלט ווי צעלאָזטער שפּיגל
מײל נאָך מײל און בײ די ראַנדן גרינט.
נאַסע שנייען זינגען אַ געזעגנס,
פֿליגלען, שפּיגלען פֿול מיט פֿאַרב און קלאַנג.
מיטן יונגן לײבנברום פֿון רעגנס
פֿלאַקערט אויף דער קינדערשער פֿאַרלאַנג
אָנצוּיאָגן אַלע ווילדע שטראָמען,
געבן זיך אַ פֿויגלדיקן טראָג
איבער מענטשן, וועלדער, פֿעלדזן, תהומען—
צו דעם נײעם, יום־טובֿדיקן טאָג!

2

With the luster from the bright green
the Irtysh sharpened by the wild rocks
wants to discover its waves again
while ice floes are starting to go. . . .
Instead of looking frightened-dark
through its one cut-out circle
it looks through its slightest waves
as the world dances in a ring
around the sun that brazenly
throws spears even as it licks
the sparkling icelight of the birch,
the way a child licks a piece of candy.

ב

מיטן שימער פֿון די העלע גרינען
שלײַפֿט זיך דער אירטיש אָן ווילד געשטיין.
ווייל די כוואַליעס זײַנע קריק געפֿינען,
ווײַלע קרײַעס האַלטן שוין אין גיין . . .
און אָנשטאָט צו קוקן שרעקיק־פֿינצטער
דורך זײַן איינעם אויסגעזעגעגטן ראָד—
קוקט ער איצט מיט כוואַליע מיט דער מינדסטער
ווי עס גייט די וועלט אַ קאַראַהאָד
רונד אַרום דער זון, וואָס אי מיט העזה
וואַרפֿט זי שווערדן, אי זי לעקט אַצינד
ס׳פֿינקלענדיקע אײַזליכט פֿון בעריאָזע,
ווי עס לעקט זײַן צוקערל אַ קינד.

35

KYRGYZ

Peace be to you, Kyrgyz, far away
by the Irtysh gilded by bonfires,
where you infold a chant
among dancing spears and lull
your sorrow, until you fall asleep.
Each one sips his lament like liquor.
And the old hump of the camel
smiles with its creases and can understand
the music of your saffron fever.
When my life flickers like a lantern,
I bend my song towards you,
open seven ears and—listen.

קירגיזן

שלום אײך אין װײטעניש, קירגיזן,
בײַם אירטיש, פֿון שטיטערן באַגילדט,
װוּ צעװישן טאַנצנדיקע שפֿיזן
װױקלט איר אַ ניגון און פֿאַרשפֿילט
אײַער אומעט, ביז איר פֿאַלט אין דרעמל.
יעדער זופֿט װי בראַנפֿן זײַן געװײן.
און דער אַלטער הױקער פֿונעם קעמל
שמײכלט מיט די קנײַטשן, קאָן פֿאַרשטײַן
די מוזיק פֿון אײַער געלן פֿיבער.
װען מײַן לעבן צאַנקט װי אַ לאָמטער,
בײַ־ג איך מײַן געזאַנג צו אײַך אַריבער,
עפֿן זײבן אױערן און—הער.

MY FRIEND TSHANGURI

I

Are you still alive, my friend Tshanguri,
or are you a snow-covered shape?
Your dear face flickers from the clouds
along with its pupils, loaned from the forest.
Come, let us play again
and find what we never had.
With the first breath of dawn
let us kiss each blade of grass and leaf,
gulp mare's milk from a skin jug
as we go off hunting owls.
Brother, after wandering so far, let us
fall asleep along the way, as we used to.

מײַן חבֿרל טשאַנגורי

א

לעבסטו נאָך, מײַן חבֿרל טשאַנגורי,
אָדער ביסט אַ שנײיִקע געשטאַלט?
פֿון די וואָלקנס פֿלעמלט מיר דײַן צורה
מיט די אַפֿלען אויסגעבאַרגט אין וואַלד.
קום זיך שפּילן ווידער און געפֿינען
וואָס מיר האָבן קיין מאָל ניט געהאַט.
מיטן ערשטן אָטעם פֿון באַגינען
לאָמיר קושן יעדער גראָז און בלאַט.
לאָמיר זשליאָקען קליאַטשעמילך פֿון לאָגל
און אויף סאָווועס מאַכן אַ געיעג.
לאָמיר, ברודער, נאָכן לאַנגן וואַגל
אײַנשלאָפֿן ווי דעמאָלט פֿאַזע וועג.

2

Come and ride again on your deaf,
humped camel—and quickly
pull me up by my little shirt—
we will fly with the wind,
and meet the birth of shadows
in quiet corners at the eve of night.
All grasses enchant and gleam.
The splendor does not recognize itself.
Specks of lives darken in the distance.
The Irtysh, mottled by clouds, glows;
the camel, bluing. And we both ride
to the glistering cliffs of granite.

קום צו ריטן ווידער אויף דין טויבן,
הויקערדיקן קעמל, און געשווינד
פֿאַרן פּיצל העמד אַ צי מיך אויבן, —
און אַוועקגעלאָזן זיך אין ווינט,
צו באַגעגענען אין שטילע ווינקלען
דעם געבורט פֿון שאָטנס ערבֿ נאַכט.
אַלע גראָזן צויבערן און פֿינקלען,
עס דערקענט אַליין זיך ניט די פּראַכט.
פֿלעקן לעבנס טונקלען אין די וויטן,
דער אירטיש, אַ וואָלקנדיקער, גליט.
ס׳בלויט דער קעמל. און מיר ביידע ריטן
צו די בלאַנקע פֿעלדזן פֿון גראַניט.

41

3

When the steep mountains disappear—
a violet forest swims into view.
A long hand of evening begins
to bind everything that hides separately.
The last flame dances on a fir tree.
The last word dances on the lips.
The camel kneels in a grass-dream.
Darker. And only stillness gleams.
A harrow cuts through damp clouds
and opens their secrets. Night comes on.
And we both eat the moon
like a sliced watermelon.

ווען די בערג די שטאָציקע פֿאַרשווינדן—
גיט אַ שווּם אַ פֿיאָלעטער וואַלד.
ס׳נעמט אַ לאַנגע אָוונטהאַנט פֿאַרבינדן
אַלצדינג וואָס באַזונדער זיך באַהאַלט.
אויף אַ יאָדלע טאַנצט דאָס לעצטע פֿלעמל.
אויף די ליפֿן טאַנצט דאָס לעצטע וואָרט.
אין אַ גראָזן־חלום קניט דער קעמל.
טונקעלער. און בלויז די שטילקייט קלאָרט.
פֿייכטן וואָלקן שנײַדט אַדורך אַ בראָנע.
עפֿנט זײַנע סודות. נאַכט קומט אָן.
און מיר עסן בײַדע די לבֿנה
ווי אַן אויפֿגעשניטענעם קאַוואָן.

BY A BONFIRE

I

A bonfire blows the night apart in the forest,
young trees turning gray from terror.
Shadows fall among crackling branches
and plants where axes flash.
And Kyrgyz—children, women, men—
gaze at the fiery brink.
Branches crackle with the crowing of roosters.
And like pearls from a broken string,
dew falls on rising sparks,
dew falls on pleading hands.
A bird—sunk in the night—
makes flight, and its violin burns.

בײַם שײַטער

א

בלאָזט די נאַכט פֿונאַנד אין וואַלד אַ שײַטער,
ווערן יונגע ביימער גראָ פֿון שרעק.
צווישן קנאַקנדיקע צווײַגן, קריטער,
פֿאַלן שאָטנס, ווו עס בליצן העק.
און קירגיזן—קינדער, פֿרויען, מענער—
שפּיגלען זיך אין זייער שאַרפֿן ראַנד.
ס׳קנאַקן צווײַגן מיטן קריי פֿון הענער.
און ווי פֿערל פֿון געפֿלאַצטן באַנד
פֿאַלט אַ טוי אויף שטײַגנדיקע פֿונקען,
פֿאַלט אַ טוי אויף בעטנדיקע הענט.
און אַ פֿויגל אין דער נאַכט פֿאַרזונקען—
קומט צו פֿליִען, און זײַן פֿידל ברענט.

45

2

Now a bronze figure offers a tremor
full of power near the flame.
Dancing with a silver bandura—
a whirl at one with the forest.
A whirl. A drumbeat. A blazing chant.
Until in the spark-rhythms of a concert—
the surroundings begin ringing and swaying,
and last stars descend into the beards.
Drunk Kyrgyz dance, dance
in a chain near a flaming table.
The Irtysh—its waves
flowing spears—tickles the horizon.

ב

איצט דערלאַנגט אַ פֿלאַטער פֿול מיט גבֿורה
לעבן פֿלאַם אַ בראָנדזענע געשטאַלט.
און אין טאַנץ מיט זילבערנער באַנדורע—
אַ געדריי צוזאַמען מיטן וואַלד.
אַ געדריי. אַ פֿויק. אַ הייסער ניגון.
ביז אין פֿונקען־ריטעם פֿון קאָנצערט—
נעמט די געגנט גלאָקיק זיך צעוויגן,
פֿאַלן לעצטע שטערן אין די בערד.
נעמען שיכּור צוטאַנצן קירגיזן
אין אַ קייט ביים פֿלאַקערדיקן טיש.
און מיט כוואַליעס, לויפֿנדיקע שפּיזן,
קיצלט האַריזאָנטן דער אירטיש.

47

NORTH STAR

North star, we stride together,
I am your snowman in a garment of skin.
Neighbors flee before my cold,
only birches remain by the fence.
North star, faithful until death,
how much mildness you awake and bring back!
Every summer, a fire snows on me,
every winter, glinting, you kling-klang in me.
May unceasing memory
be drawn to your blue smile.
May its sounds, claim,
remain over me my monument.

1936

48

צפֿון־שטערן

צפֿון־שטערן, שפּאַנסט מיט מיר מיר אין איינעם,
כ׳בין דײַן שנײַמענטש אין אַ קלײד פֿון הויט.
פֿאַר מײַן קעלט צעלויפֿן זיך די שכנים,
בלויז בעריאָזעס בלײַבן לעבן פֿלויט.
צפֿון־שטערן, בײַזן טויט געטרײַער,
וויפֿל מילדקייט וועקסטו און דערמאָנסט!
אַלע זומער שנײַט אויף מיר אַ פֿײַער,
אַלע ווינטער גלינסטו מיר און גלאָנסט.
זאָל די ניט־פֿאַרגאַנגענע דערמאָנונג,
צו דײַן בלאָען שמייכל זײַן געווענדעט.
זאָלן אָט די קלאַנגען, זאָל די מאָנונג,
בלײַבן איבער מיר אַ מאָנומענט.

1936

A Haystack

My head on a silvery haystack, like a pillow,
I doze in a meadow. No, I'm awake.
As many stars overhead—as drops
of blessed dew on the earth. A white dirt road
ascends in my fixed eyes,
and this very haystack, where I lie,
resembles my fate, is dear to me
and slowly rocks me to sleep in its cradle.

Redolence of blood like blooming honey.
The raw plain reeks with hot desire.
The haystack lies in its dew, in its moonlight,
and I—it seems to me, I lie near myself
and in the fresh hay breathe the aroma
of green time. I feel through myself the course
of flower and scythe. I lie on a sacrificial altar
of colors, odors. Each rustle and sound
becomes strangely near, streams through my limbs;
the least floret, blade of grass arouses ache . . .
I lie in hay—a wanderer, tired,
until I myself become a haystack.

1936

אַ סקירדע היי

מיט זילבערלעכער סקירדע היי צוקאָפּנס,
איך דרימל אויף אַ לאָנקע. ניין, איך וואַך.
אַזוי פֿיל שטערן אויבן—וויפֿל טראָפּנס
געבענטשטער טוי אויף דר׳ערד. אַ וויסער שליאַך
גייט אויף אין מײַנע גליווערדיקע אויגן,
און אָט די סקירדע היי, אַװוּ איך ליג,
דערמאָנט מיר אין מײַן גורל, איז מיר אייגן
און וויגט מיך אײַן פֿאַװואָליע אין איר וויג.

געֿרוך פֿון בלוט ווי בליענדיקער האָניק.
עס שלאָגט מיט דער הייסער לוסט דער רויער פּליין.
די סקירדע היי ליגט טוייק און לבָניק,
און איך—מיר דאַכט, איך ליג לעם זיך אַליין
און אָטעם אײַן אין פֿרישן היי דעם ריח
פֿון גרינער צײַט. איך שפּיר דורך זיך דעם גאַנג
פֿון בלום און קאָסע. כ׳ליג אויף אַ מזבח
פֿון פֿאַרבן, ריחות. יעדער שאָרך און קלאַנג
ווערט מאָדנע נאָענט, שטראָמט דורך מײַנע גלידער;
דאָס מינדסטע בלימל, גרעזל טוט מיר וויי...
איך ליג אין היי—אַ וואַנדערער אַ מידער,
ביז וואַנען כ׳ווער אַליין אַ סקירדע היי.

1936

Ant Nest

Ant nest, forest-underlife,
shattered by my curious poke,
your labyrinths, layer after layer,
fallen into dust—look,
my head falls and cracks open,
teeming with ants—words.

And each word—up, down and over,
from nerve to nerve, through serums
and spheres, then scurrying from crannies
with little white eggs in their mouths.

1940

מוראַשקע־נעסט

מוראַשקע־נעסט, דו וואַלדס אונטערבאַוווסטזײַן,
צעגישטערט פֿון אַ נײַגעריקן שטאָק,——
מיט לאַבירינטן דײַנע, שטאָק נאָך שטאָק
צעפֿאַלענע אין שטויב, זאָל דיר באַוווסט זײַן:
ווי דו בין איך. מײַן שאַרבן פֿאַלט. אָט ווערט ער
צעטראָגן פֿון מוראַשקעלעך——פֿון ווערטער.

און יעדער וואָרט——אַרויף, אַראָפּ, אַריבער,
פֿון נערוו צו נערוו, דורך רויך און קוויל.
און אַלע יאָגן פֿון די שטיבער
מיט ווײַסן אייעלע אין מויל.

1940

Poems to a Sleepwalker

1

I have known you for a long time now,
    since you were an amphibian.
I still remember the primal state of sin:
    "Do you love me?"—"Yes, I love you."

We coupled
    under silvery downpours.
And our love for each other
    grew before our very eyes.

2

You sweep the dust out of my dream
with a silver broom.
The room becomes clean. A branch of lilac
greets the room through the windowpane.

And your hand, which you stretch to anoint me,
smooths out the furrows in my forehead
just as your pleated nightgown
buttons your breast to a star.

לידער צו אַ לונאַטיקערין

איך קען דיך פֿון לאַנג שוין, פֿון זינט
ביסט געווען אַן אַמפֿיביע.
געדענק נאָך די ערשטקייט פֿון זינד:
האָסט מיך ליב?—איך האָב ליב, יע.

מיר האָבן זיך ביידע געפֿאָרט
אונטער זילבערנע שלאָקסן.
און אונדזער פֿאַרליבטשאַפֿט איז דאָרט
ווי אויף הייוון געוואַקסן.

מיט אַ זילבערנעם בעזעם
קערסטו אויס פֿון מײַן חלום די שטויבן.
ווערט דאָס צימערל ריין. דורך די שויבן
גריסט אַ צוויצגעלע בעז אים.

און דײַן האַנט, וואָס דו שטרעקסט מיך צו זאַלבן,
פֿרעסט די קנייטשעלעך אויס אויף מײַן שטערן,
ווי דײַן נאַכטהעמד אין פֿאַלבן
וואָס פֿאַרקנעפּלט דײַן ברוסט אויף אַ שטערן.

3

I only want to touch your secret like a sail
bent by a storm, touched by the billows—
a secret, the path to it
sealed off by the wax of sin.

That's the place of my desire. I must finally
set eyes on the landscape that frightens and calms.
Your secret, like the tonespirit in a violin's f-holes,
must start to quaver from my soaring blood.

4

Who is he, the third one, who raises
a storm as soon as I caress you?
It is he—your lover, the man in the moon,
who reigns from a silver throne
on the darkest branch in the forest.

We cannot make a threesome
because quicksilver cools the passion.
My body quivers from envy
when the man in the moon sips out the pupil of your eye
and kisses your path with pearls.

Choose one or the other. Choose.
Drive away the second one, the loser.
Or, turn a mite into even more of a mite,
and burn him in a bonfire of silver,
you bird, you dream, you wife!

1940

ג

איך וויל בלויז באַרירן דײַן סוד ווי אַ זעגל,
געבויגן פֿון שטורעם, באַרירט דאָס געאיינד—
אַ סוד, וואָס צו אים איז פֿאַרזיגלט דאָס שטעגל
מיט טריוואַקס פֿון זינד.

אַהין איז מײַן גלוסט. איך מוז געבן אַן עפֿן
דערזען דעם פֿייזאַזש וואָס דערשרעקט און באַרוט.
דײַן סוד, ווי דער טאָנגײַסט אין פֿידלשע עפֿן
מוז ווערן באַפֿאָכט פֿון מײַן פֿליגלדיק בלוט.

ד

ווער איז ער, דער דריטער, וואָס באַלד
ווי כ׳צערטל דיך מאַכט ער אַ גוואַלד?
ס׳איז דאָך ער—דײַן געליבטער **לָבָניק**.
וואָס רעגירט אויף אַ זילבערן טראָניק
אויף טונקלסטן צווײַגל פֿון וואַלד.

מיר קענען ניט זײַן זאַלבע דריט
ווען קווערקזילבער קילט דאָס געבליט.
ס׳גיט מײַן לײַב זיך פֿון קינאה אַ צאַפֿל
ווען לבָניק זופֿט אויס דײַן שוואַרצאַפֿל
און באַקושט דיר מיט פּערל די טריט.

קלײַב איינעם פֿון ביידן אויס, קלײַב.
דעם צוווייטן שלימזל פֿאַרטרײַב.
אָדער מאַך פֿון אַ מילב אים נאָך מילבער,
און פֿאַרברען אים אין שײַטער פֿון זילבער,
דו פֿויגל, דו חלום, דו ווײַב!

1940

57

Two Bullets

1

I know a man, hit by a bullet
that sticks in his breast—a bird in a bit of sun.
How strange! Among the swarm of people
he, perhaps, is the most powerful son.

And he loves his bullet. Instead of killing him
it captured and wounded death,
melted life's chains like snow
and animated untouched ground.

2

Also, leaping from a battle, a bullet
sticks in me—loaded with poems.
And when I am sick like an indoor plant at night—
it burns out the poison in my limbs.
And I love my bullet. Its hot crucible
melts the world. From its metal I mold,
create my truth, the way a child in a crib
forms his planet from pure nothing.

1940

צוויי קוילן

א

איך קען אַ מאַן, געטראָפֿן האָט אַ קויל אים
און שטעקט אים אין ברוסט,—אַ פֿויגל אין אַ שטיקל זון.
ווי אויסטערליש! צעווישן גאָר דעם עולם
איז ער, קען זײַן, דער גבֿורההדיקסטער זון.

און ער האָט ליב זײַן קויל. אַנשטאָט אים טייטן
האָט זי דעם טויט געפֿאַנגען און פֿאַרוווּנדט.
צעשמאָלצן ווי אַ שניי דעם לעבנס קייטן
און אויפֿגעלעבט אַ ניט־באַרירטן גרונט.

ב

אויך אין מיר, פֿאַרשפּרונגען פֿון אַ שלאַכט
שטעקט אַ קויל,—געלאָדן פֿול מיט לידער.
און בין איך קראַנק ווי אַ וואַזאָן בײַ נאַכט—
ברענט זי אַרויס דעם סם פֿון מײַנע גלידער.
און איך האָב ליב מײַן קויל. איר הייסער טיגל
צעשמעלצט די וועלט. פֿון איר מעטאַל איך קנעט,
באַשאַף מײַן אמת, ווי אַ קינד אין וויגל
קנעט אַרויס פֿון לויטער גאָרנישט זײַן פּלאַנעט.

1940

In the Cell

Without a doubt: this darkness wants to choke me!
The leaden mice gnaw out my glances.
I shake in the cell and sink between walls:
If only there were something human and familiar.

I unexpectedly come across a piece of glass, where
the moon twitches, caught in pincers of glass.
I forget that I'm sinking while I'm harnessed in fever:
this, after all, was shaped by a human hand!

I clasp the moon in its glassy edge:
"Do you want to? I give my life to you as a gift!"
Only life is hot and the glass—a cold thing
and it's a shame to take it to my throat . . .

Vilna, end of June, 1941

אין קאַרצער

ניט אַנדערש: די פינצטערניש וויל מיך דערשטיקן!
די בלינענע מיז גרינזשען אויס מיינע בליקן.
איך וואַרף זיך אין קאַרצער און זינק צווישן ווענט:
וואָלט עפּעס געווען וואָס איז מענטשלעך, באקענט.

דערטאַפּ איך אַ שטיקעלע גלאָז, ווו געפּאַנגען
עס צוקט די לבנה אין גלעזערנע צוואַנגען.
פאַרגעס איך מיין זינקען אין פיבער געשפּאַנט:
—דאָס האָט דאָך באַשאַפּן אַ מענטשישע האַנט!

און כ׳צערטל אין גלאָזיקער שאַרף די לבנה:
—,,דו ווילסט? כ׳גיב מיין לעבן דיר אָפּ אַ מתנה!״
נאָר ס׳לעבן איז הייס און דאָס גלעזל—אַ קאַלטס
און ס׳איז מיר אַ שאָד עס צו נעמען צום האַלדז . . .

ווילנע, סוף יוני 1941

I Lie in a Coffin

I lie in a coffin,
as if in wooden clothes.
I lie.
Call it a little ship
on stormy waves,
call it a cradle.

And here,
where bodies
have parted from time,
I call you, my sister,
and you hear me call
from far away.

What unexpected body
is quivering in a coffin?
You come.
I recognize the pupil of your eye,
your breath,
your light.

Apparently that is the plan:
today here,
tomorrow there,
and now in a coffin,
as if in wooden clothes,
my word keeps on singing.

Vilna, August 30, 1941

איך ליג אין אַן אָרון

איך ליג אין אַן אָרון
ווי אין הילצערנע קליידער,
איך ליג.
זאָל זײַן, ס׳איז אַ שיפֿל
אויף שטורמישע כוואַליעס,
זאָל זײַן, ס׳איז אַ וויג.

און דאָ,
ווו עס האָבן זיך גופֿן
געשיידט מיט דער צײַט,
רוף איך דיך, שוועסטער,
און דו הערסט מײַן רופֿן
אין ווײַט.

וואָס טוט זיך אין אָרון אַ צאַפּל
אַ ליב אומגעריכט?
דו קומסט.
איך דערקען דײַן שוואַרצאַפּל,
דײַן אָטעם,
דײַן ליכט.

אַזוי איז אַ פֿנים דער סדר:
הײַנט דאָ,
מאָרגן דאָרט,
און איצט אין אַן אָרון,
ווי אין הילצערנע קליידער,
זינגט אַלץ נאָך מײַן וואָרט.

ווילנע, 30סטן אויגוסט 1941

63

From a Lost Poem

Mama,
I'm sick.
My soul, scabby, and,
maybe,
even more,
a yellowmadness.
And the heal-all of your kiss
is too holy
even to inspire
the source of my wounds.

But if it's true
you love me, as always
second only to God,
my last plea and commandment is:
Choke me!
Choke with those very fingers,
motherly fingers,
that played along
my willow cradle.

פֿון אַ פֿאַרלוירענער פּאָעמע

מאַמע,

כ׳בין קראַנק.

מײַן נשמה איז קרעציק.

און אפֿשר נאָך מער:

ס׳איז אַ געלער שגעון.

און דער זאַלב פֿון דײַן קוש

איז צו הייליק, ער זאָל

מיר באַהויכן צו מאָל

מײַנע וווּנדיקע דנאָען.

נאָר אויב דאָס איז וואָר,

אַז דו ליבסט מיך ווי שטענדיק

דעם צווייטן נאָך גאָט—

איז מײַן לעצטער געבעט און געבאָט:

—דערשטיק מיך!

דערשטיק מיט די מאַמישע פֿינגער

וואָס האָבן געשפּילט

אויף מײַן ווערבענעם וויגל.

65

Will mean
to me, your love is strong, like death;
will mean
to me, you entrusted your love;
and I will turn
into before-my-birth
and be and not be
like a star
in water.

Vilna Ghetto

וועט מײנען:

דײן ליבשאַפֿט איז שטאַרק ווי דער טויט.

וועט מײנען:

דו האָסט מיר דײן ליבשאַפֿט פֿאַרטרויט.

און איך וועל פֿאַרקערן

אין איידער־מײַן־ווערן

און זײַן און ניט זײַן

ווי אַ שטערן

אין וואַסער.

ווילנער געטאָ

Every Hour, Every Day

Every hour, every day—
no longer an hour,
no longer a day;
it is a prepared sacrificial altar in your bones,
where everything that you feel, that you see,
is devoured,
and yet at the same time you sing
when you devour yourself.

Vilna Ghetto, April 27, 1943

יעדער שעה, יעדער טאָג

יעדער שעה, יעדער טאָג,—
איז מער ניט קיין שעה,
איז מער ניט קיין טאָג,
ס׳איז אַ גרייטער מזבח בײַ דיר אין געביין,
ווּ פֿאַרשלונגען ווערט אַלץ, וואָס דו פֿילסט, וואָס דו זעסט,
און דו זינגסט נאָך דערבײַ, ווען דו פֿרעסט
זיך אַליין.

ווילנער געטאָ, 27סטן אַפריל 1943

The Burial

Night at the Zaretshe cemetery.
It is raining, and birds fall from ruined nests.
Flashing strings cover the area.
Tombstones burn in the rain. And Esther—
among the graves. With her nails she scratches
the bony earth and with her shoulder screens
the downpour. Her dress like a sail in a storm.
No remedy for the cloudburst.
The deeper she digs, the fuller the tiny grave.
The face of death is in the crazed rain.

Fortifying the grave all around with loam,
she slap-dashedly scoops out the water.
And unwraps, secretly, from a bundle a child.
In the flashing, wet night, a small corpse,
the size of an arm, starts to shine,
washed clean by the rain for the burial.
A *minyan* of graves comes to mourn,
overgrown with boards like wooden flowers.
The rain becomes quieter, now the tiny child
is swaddled in shrouds—a white diaper.

די קבֿורה

ביי נאַכט אויף זאַרעטשער בית־עלמין. עס רעגנט,
און פֿייגעלעך פֿאַלן פֿון חרובֿע נעסטער.
מיט בליציקע סטרונעס באַצוויגן די געגנט.
עס ברענען אין רעגן מצבֿות. און אסתּר—
צעווישן די קבֿרים. זי רייסט מיט די נעגל
די ביניקע ערד און פֿאַרשטעלט מיט דער פֿלייצע
דעם שלאַקס. איר געקלייד, ווי אין שטורעם אַ זעגל.
ניטאָ פֿאַרן קוואַליקן וואַסער קיין עצה.
וואָס טיפֿער זי גראָבט, ווערט דאָס קבֿרל פֿולער.
דאָס פּנים פֿון טויט איז דער רעגן דער דולער.

באַפֿעסטיקט דעם קבֿר אַרום און אַרומיק
מיט ליים—נעמט זי אויסשעפּן אייליק דאָס וואַסער.
און וויקלט אַרויס אין געהיים פֿון אַ קלומיק
אַ קינד. אין דער נאַכט אין דער בליציקער, נאַסער,
נעמט ליציכטן אַ מתל, די גרייס ווי אַן אָרעם.
זי איז עס מטהר אין רעגן. עס קומען
אַהער צו באַקלאָגן אַ מנין מיט קבֿרים,
באַוואַקסן מיט ברעטלעך ווי הילצערנע בלומען.
דער רעגן ווערט שטילער, אַצינד איז דאָס קינדל
פֿאַרהילט אין תּכריכים—אַ וויסינקער ווינדל.

71

She lovingly brings it to the grave: "Sleep calmly!"
(The way one brings a child to *kheyder* for the first time.)
A bolt of lightning reveals a Jewish letter
here and there; it unveils the cemetery.
Maybe the archangel Gabriel will come and throw in
a gold coin? He doesn't. Covered over.
A drunken flash shows her the distance
back to the sewer, in clouded shadows.
She plucks up a bunch of grass along the way
and wails, a goodbye; and wails, a goodbye.

From *Secret City,* 1945–47

זי ברענגט עס מיט ליבשאַפֿט אין קבֿר: שלאָף רויִק!
(אַזוי ווי אַ קינד ס׳ערשטע מאָל אין חדר).
אַ בליק ווייזט אַ ייִדישן אות ווי־ניט־ווייק,
ער איז דעם בית־עלמינס אַנטפּלעקער, באַשיידער.
און אפֿשר וועט קומען גבֿריאל־המלאך
און וואַרפֿן אַ רענדל? ער וואַרפֿט ניט. פֿאַרשאָטן.
אַ שיכּורער בליק ווייזט איר אָן דעם מהלך
צוריק צום קאַנאַל, אין באַוואָלקנטן שאָטן.
אַ בינטעלע גראָז פֿליקט זי אַף אונטער וועגנס
און ברומט אַ געזאַנגס, און ברומט אַ געזאַנגנס.

73

To the Thin Vein on My Head

I fully entrust myself to the thin vein on my head.
My word is nourished in the crystalline song of the dust.
And all the seven wisdoms the whirlwind sows
fall, without wings, like hail on a windowpane.

I love the unadulterated taste of a word, that won't betray
    itself,
not some sweet-and-sour hybrid with a strange taste.
Whether I rise on the rungs of my ribs, or fall—
that word is mine. In the black pupil of death—a little flame.

No matter how great my generation might be—greater yet is
    its smallness.
Still eternal is the word in all of its ugliness and splendor.
To the thin vein on my head, I entrust ultimate beauty:
A wind. A clump of grass. The last star in the night.

1945

צום דינעם אָדערל אין קאָפּ

צום דינעם אָדערל אין קאָפּ פֿאַרטרוי איך זיך אין גאַנצן.
מײַן וואָרט זיך נערט אין זײַן קרישטאָליק־זינגעגנדיקן שטויב.
און אַלע זיבן חכמות, וואָס דער ווירבל וויל פֿאַרפֿלאַנצן—
זיי פֿאַלן אָפּ אַנטפּליגלטע ווי האָגל אָן אַ שויב.

איך ליב דאָס וואָרט וואָרט פֿון אײַן געשמאַק, וואָס זאָל אין זיך ניט פֿאַלשן,
און ניט קיין זיס־און־זויערן היבריד מיט פֿרעמדן טעם.
אַלץ איינס, צי שטײַג איך הויך אַרויף מײַנע ריפּן צי איך פֿאַל שוין—
דאָס וואָרט איז מײַנס. אין שוואַרצאַפּל פֿון טויט—אַ שטיקל פֿלאַם.

ווי גרויס עס זאָל ניט זײַן זײַן מײַן דור—איז גרעסער נאָך זײַן קליינקייט.
נאָר אייביק איז דאָס וואָרט מיט גאָר זײַן מיאוסקייט און פּראַכט.
צום דינעם אָדערל אין קאָפּ פֿאַרטרוי איך לעצטע שיינקייט:
אַ ווינט. אַ בינטל גראָז. דעם לעצטן שטערן פֿון דער נאַכט.

1945

The Woman of Marble in Père Lachaise

The woman
of marble in Père Lachaise
snared me.
It was like this:
I went to Père Lachaise
with a fresh sprig of lilac
for the remains of Chopin
turned into sounds.

The very name of the place
where the master was born—
written into the stone—
made me shudder.
When you consider the place,
he was almost a brother.
And the time?
What's a century
compared with our minutes?
God knows, I don't covet our meager present.
I put my ear to the stone
and heard: a piano raining there.

די פֿרוי פֿון מירמל אויפֿן פֿער־לאַשעז

די פֿרוי
פֿון מירמל אויפֿן פֿער־לאַשעז
האָט מיך געפֿאַנגען.
עס איז געוואָרן אַזוי:
איך בין געגאַנגען
אויף פֿער־לאַשעז,
מיט פֿרישן בינטל בעז,
אים צו דערלאַנגען
שאָפֿענס געביין
פֿאַרוואַנדלטן אין קלאַנגען.

שוין דאָס אַליין,
וואָס אויפֿן שטיין
איז אָנגעשריבן ווי דער
מײַסטער איז געבוירן—
האָט געטאָן מיך אַ צערודער.
ווערליק אָרט איז ער כּמעט אַ ברודער.
און ווערליק צײַט?—
נאָר וואָס איז אַ יאָרהונדערט
אין פֿאַרגלײַך מיט אונדזערע מינוטן?
אָסור, אויב איך בין מײַן פֿיצל איצטיקייט מקנא!
איך האָב מײַן אויער צוגעגלײַגט צום שטיין
און דערהערט: עס רעגנט דאָרט אַ פֿיאַנע.

77

Only then, my amazed ear
felt a warm quiver,
a stirring.
I raise my head—
a woman-monument bends down to me.
The woman-monument come to life,
awake,
opens her lips of green mold.
She sticks her hand into my forelock
and pelts my face with her stone-speech:

> "The heart I guard
> left long ago for its homeland.
> Only his dust blooms
> in this red, dead loam.
>
> But if you really want, monsieur,
> to expend your life, like my master Chopin—
> have you the slightest idea
> where your heart should be taken?"

נאָר דעמאָלט האָט מײַן גאָפֿנדיקער אויער
דערשפּירט אַ וואָרעם צאָפּלען,
אַ באַועגן.
אַ הייב דעם קאָפּ—
אַ פֿרוי־מצבֿה בייגט זיך מיר אַנטקעגן.

די פֿרוי־מצבֿה אויפֿגעלעבט און וואָך,
צעעפֿנט ליפֿן אָנגעשימלט־גרינע.
זי שטעקט אַרײַן איר האַנט אין מײַן טשופּערינע
און שטײַנערט מיר אין פּנים אויף איר שפּראַך:

,,דאָס הארץ פֿון דעם וואָס איך היט
איז לאַנג אַוועק אין זײַן היימלאַנד.
און בלויז דער שטויב זײַנער בליט
אין רויטן, טויטן ליימלאַנד.

נאָר דו אַז דו ווילסט, מעסיע,
ווי מײַן האַר שאָפֿען פֿאַרברענגען,—
צי ווײַסטו ווו נײַן, ווו יע,
מע זאָל דאָס האַרץ דײַנס ברענגען?''

The sun shrank in my sprig of lilac,
went out.
I turned numb in Père Lachaise,
speechless:
Was it worth it to count up
some thirty years,
losing those dear to me,
hanging by a hair,
emerging from the ovens
with unburnt tears
only to hear just now at Père Lachaise
that my strong heart isn't even worth a sou?
And if I were to make a will
so someone should bring my heart home—
the entire Diaspora,
the sad Diaspora—
          will laugh.

Paris, 1947

די זון האָט אין מײַן צוזיגל בעז

פֿאַרשרומפּן זיך, פֿאַרלאָשן.

געבליבן בין איך אויפֿן פֿער־לאַשעז

געליימט. אָן לשון:

כּדאַי געווען צו זאַמלען אויף מײַן קאָנטע

דרײַסיק יאָר,

פֿאַרלירן אַלע נאָנטע,

בלײַבן הענגען אויף אַ האָר,

אַרויסגיין פֿונעם קאַלכאויוון

מיט ניט־פֿאַרברענטע טרערן,

אַז איך זאָל איצט, אויף פֿער־לאַשעז דערהערן,

אַז מײַן אַלמאַכטיק האַרץ איז ווערט אַ פּיים.

און אויב איך וועל מיר אַ צוואה מאַכן

מע זאָל שפּעטער ברענגען עס אַהיים—

וועט גאָר דאָס טרויעריקע וועלטפֿאָלק—לאַכן.

פּאַריז 1947

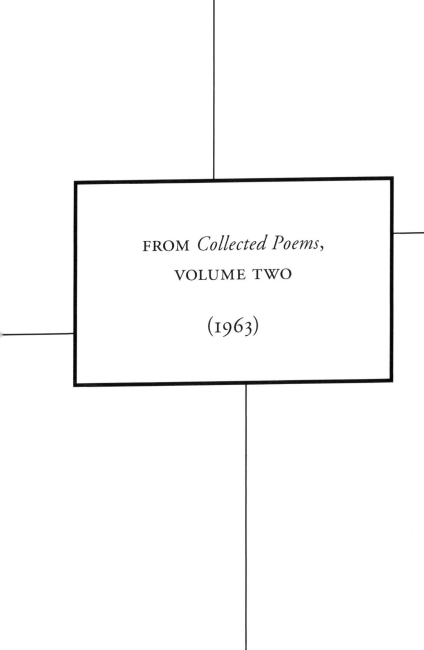

FROM *Collected Poems,*
VOLUME TWO

(1963)

Deer by the Red Sea

The sunset, stubborn and brazen,
remains in the Red Sea at night,
when pink deer, innocent, gentle, come
to the palace of water to quench their thirst.

They leave their silk shadows on the shore,
and their long fiddle-faces lick
rings of coolness in the Red Sea,
and there they become engaged to silence.

Finished, they run away. Rose-flecks
animate the sand. But the sunset-deer,
mournful, remain in the water, and lick
the silence of those no longer there.

1949

הירשן ביים ים־סוף

דער זונפֿאַרגאַנג האָט זיך פֿאַרעקשנט מיט העזה
צו בלײַבן אין ים־סוף ביז נאַכט, װען עס קומען
צום פּאַלאַץ פֿון װאַסער—די אומשולדיק ראַזע,
די איידעלע הירשן צו שטילן דעם גומען.

זיי לאָזן די זײַדענע שאָטנס ביים באָרטן
און לעקן אין ים־סוף די רינגען פֿון קילקייט
מיט פֿידלענע פּנימער לאַנגע. און דאָרטן
געשעט די פֿאַרקנסונג בײַ זיי מיט דער שטילקייט.

געענדיקט—אַנטלויפֿן זיי. רויזיקע פֿלעקן
באַלעבן דעם זאַמד. נאָר עס בלײַבן פֿול יאַמער
די זונפֿאַרגאַנג־הירשן אין װאַסער און לעקן
די שטילקייט פֿון יענע, װאָס זענען ניטאָ מער.

1949

Denkmol nokh a ferd

(Memorial for a Horse)

A horse with a red soul
and with two nightingale-eyes
revealed itself in the snow, like an angel,
and halted, breathless—in the snow.

Let us remember this horse,
before the snows melt.

Wolves could not overtake him
nor glaring snowdrifts blind him
until the rider, that naked boy,
brought him from the enemy's lines.

Let us remember the horse,
before the snows melt.

The rider kneeling before his deliverer,
as if they were dreaming together . . .
and later shaped a memorial—
a horse shaped of snow.

Let us remember the horse,
before the snows melt.

And everyone saw that wonder,
how the red soul of death
arrived under that snowy hide—
in that horse, shaped of snow.

That horse, remember that horse,
before the snow melts.

דענקמאָל נאָך אַ פֿערד

אַזאַ פֿערד מיט אַ רויטער נשמה
און מיט אויגן ווי צוויי סאַלאָוויייען,
האָט אַנטפֿלעקט זיך אין וואַלד ווי אַ מלאך
און געבליבן אָן אָטעם—אין שנייען.

לאָמיר געדענקען דעם פֿערד,
איידער די שנייען צעגייען.

ס׳האָבן וועלף ניט געקאָנט אים דעריאָגן,
און פֿאַרבלענדן—די בלאָנקע זאָוויייען,
ביז דעם רײַטער, דעם נאַקעטן יינגל,
אונדז געבראַכט פֿון דעם שׂונאס אַרמייען.

לאָמיר געדענקען דעם פֿערד,
איידער די שנייען צעגייען.

האָט דער רײַטער געקניט לעבן רעטער,
ווי זיי וואָלטן געחלומט אין צווייען . . .
און געקנאַטן אים שפּעטער אַ דענקמאָל,
אַזאַ פֿערד אויסגעקנאָטן פֿון שנייען.

לאָמיר געדענקען דעם פֿערד,
איידער די שנייען צעגייען.

און געזען האָבן אַלע דעם ווונדער,
ווי די רויטע נשמה פֿון טויטן
איז אַרײַן אונטער שנייייקע הויטן—
אינעם פֿערד, וואָס געקנאָטן פֿון שנייען.

לאָמיר געדענקען דעם פֿערד,
איידער די שנייען צעגייען.

Blackberries

"Hungry ones: Let's pick
blackberries in the night."
Is it something to make note of:
Blackberries in the night?

Dark. Only the yellow owl
plays cards with the night.
The fir trees in the forests—
blackberries like night.

Bent over in threesomes
toward the berries of the night,
a gang with weapons
goes to pick berries in the night.

People, used to *killing*—
kneel before a blade of grass at night,
because blackberries enchant
like flutes in the night.
And the glowworms escort,
and the yellow owl—laughs.

שוואַרצע יאַגדעס

—,,הונגעריקע! לאָמיר קלײַבן
שוואַרצע יאַגדעס אין דער נאַכט".
ס׳איז אַן אײנפֿאַל צו פֿאַרשרײַבן:
שוואַרצע יאַגדעס אין דער נאַכט?

פֿינצטער. בלויז די געלע סאָווע
שפּילט אין קאָרטן מיט דער נאַכט.
אין די וועלדער די יאָדלאָווע—
שוואַרצע יאַגדעס ווי די נאַכט.

אײַנגעבויגענע אין דרײַען
צו די יאַגדעס פֿון דער נאַכט,
גײט אַ מחנה מיט כּלי-זײַן
קלײַבן יאַגדעס אין דער נאַכט.

מענטשן, אײַנגעווווינט צו **טײטן**—
קניען פֿאַר אַ גראָז בײַ נאַכט.
ווײַל עס צויבערן ווי פֿלײטן
שוואַרצע יאַגדעס אין דער נאַכט.
און די גליווערעם באַגלײטן,
און די געלע סאָווע—לאַכט.

89

Trained Animals

Words, words! Trained animals in cages,
I set you free. Run back to the jungle, sweet slaves!
Anonymous new hymns—veins of silence,
lure me with their still unrevealed sex.

I will find among desert cliffs
that alphabet without words to be understood
by locusts and rain. What an enormous revelation:
The dead will answer and a stone will smile!

Minerals and matter will read my poetry, and fires,
that by consuming something else, turn to ash.
—Hey, Rimbaud, you conjurer and splitter of vowels,
answer, my boy: What's all this to-do about you? . . .

אויסדרעסירטע חיות

ווערטער, ווערטער! אויסדרעסירטע חיות הינטער שטײגן,
כ׳לאָז אײך פֿרײ. אַנטלױפֿט צוריק אין דזשונגל, זיסע קנעכט!
קײנעממסדיקע נײע הימנען—אָדערן פֿון שװײגן,
ציען מיך מיט זײער ניט־אַנטזיגלטן געשלעכט.

אױסגעפֿינען װעל איך צװישן מידברדיקע סקאַלעס
יענעם אלף־בית אָן װערטער, װאָס אים זאָל פֿאַרשטײן
הײשעריק און רעגן. סאַראַ גװאַלדיקע התגלות:
טױטע װעלן ענטפֿערן און שמײכלען װעט אַ שטײן!

לײענען מײן דיכטונג װעלן שטאָפֿן, מינעראַלן,
פֿײערן, װאָס עסנדיק אַ צװײיטן—װערן אַש.
הײ, רעמבאָ, דו צױבערער און שפֿאַלטער פֿון װאָקאַלן,
ענטפֿער, ייִנגל: װאָס איז דאָרט מיט דיר אַזאַ מין רעש? . . .

91

A Poem without a Name

Redfooted—
death-length, you stepped towards me
among the moist wild strawberries,
through dark-high forests—
you approached without expression, without a face . . .

A burning mirror pours out from my memory.
I drink my tearpotion, that you induced.
Each little drop has its own separate, solemn taste.
The fermenting pain of the residue comes closer. Closer.
I drink my own tearpotion and—
am I mad or drunk?
My eye a victim of your stare,
your lip—my lip.
Good morning, face:
The little drop of blood, my kiss, behind time's shutter,
is lively and my death-kin.
Each of our mouths clamped to one of her nipples—
warmth, sweet drops;
my first murder in life,
committed near a river, near the gate of Paradise.

אַ ליד אָן אַ נאָמען

רווטפֿיסיק—
ווײל טויט-לאַנג דו ביסט צו מיר געגאַנגען
צעווישן פֿײכטע פֿאַזשעמקעס,
דורך טונקל-הויכע וועלדער—
גענענסטו אָן אַ פּנים, אָן אַ פּנים . . .

אַ ברענענדיקער שפּיגל גיסט זיך אויס פֿון מײן זכרון.
איך טרינק מײן אייגן טרערגעטראַנק, וואָס דו האָסט אים באַשאַפֿן.
ס׳האָט יעדער קאַפּליע אַ באַזונדער פֿיצערלעכן טעם.
דער יויִרנדיקער ווײטיק אויפֿן דנאָ קומט נענטער, נענטער.
איך טרינק מײן אייגן טרערגעטראַנק און—
בין איך דול צי שיכּור?
ס׳געבויירט אַן אויג—אַן אויג;
אַ ליפּ—אַ ליפּ;
גוט-מאָרגן, פּנים!
דער קליינער טראָפּן בלוט, מײן קוש, אַהינטער צײטנס לאָדן
איז לעבעדיק און טױטלעך-אייגן.
צוגענאָפּלט בין איך
צום זיסן טראָפּן וואַרעמקייט,
מײן ערשטן מאָרד אין לעבן,
באַגאַנגען בײ אַ שמאָלן טײך, בײם טויער פֿון גן-עדן.

93

The river later drowned itself.
A startled wave escaped, and rolled
out from its confined current, and it will never
be older than its sixteen years.

My speech is your muteness I cut apart into words—
Conjured—and send back to their source.
But only that pulsing vein in my temple—those words you
     occupy—
confers my ceaseless expiring joy.

Since the words can't return to their source,
you disappear, without expression, without
a *bruder's* face. I
covet the bed of your grave.
Redfooted—
death-length, you stepped towards me
among the moist wild strawberries,
through dark-high forests

דער טײַך האָט שפּעטער זיך אַליין דערטרונקען.

אַנטרונען איז אַ כװאַליע אַ דערשראָקענע. אַ כװאַליע

אַרויסגעקײַקלט פֿון איר שטרענגן שטראָם. און זי װעט קיין מאָל

ניט עלטער װערן אין מײַן האַרץ, פֿון אירע זעכצן יאָר.

מײַן לשון איז דײַן שטומקייט, װאָס איך שנײַד פֿונאַנד אין װערטער

באַשװאָרענע—איך שיק זיי אָפּ צוריק צו זייער מקור.

און בלויז דער אָדערקלאַפּ אין שלייף, אַז דו האָסט זיי פֿאַרנומען,

באַלוינט מײַן גסיסהדיקע פֿרייד מיט אומטויט.

נאָר אַז די װערטער קומען ניט צוריק צו זייער מקור—

פֿאַרשװוינדסטו אָן אַ פּנים, אָן אַ פּנים.

רויטפֿיסיק—

װײַל טויט־לאַנג דו ביסט צו מיר געגאַנגען

צעװוישן פֿײַכטע פֿאָזשעמקעס,

דורך טונקל־חוישכע װעלדער.

און בלויז דײַן קבֿר בין איך אייפֿערזיכטיק—

Gather me from the ledge of time;
nest in me, like letters from a burning *siddur*.
Gather me together—I will become myself,
alone with you—our bodies entwined.

Find me in a grave, between this world and the next,
wondering which world is better . . .
Find me set on revenge for a single tear,
cooling my hot knife in the snow.

Think, that cloud darkens with my remains;
it bursts, with my face flashing down below.
Gather me together—I will become myself,
alone with you—our bodies entwined.

פֿאַרזאַמל מיך פֿון אַלע העקן צײט, פֿון שטאָק און שטײן,
פֿאַרטוליע מיך, ווי אותיות פֿון אַ ברענענדיקן סידור.
פֿאַרזאַמל־מיך־צוזאַמען—איך זאָל קענען זײַן אַלײן,
אַלײן מיט דיר, און דו—אין מײַנע גלידער.

געפֿין מיך אין אַ קבֿר צווישן יענער וועלט און דער,
בײַם איבערוועגן, וואָסער וועלט איז בעסער . . .
געפֿין מיך בײַם נקמה־נעמען פֿאַר אַ האַלבער טרער,
און ווען דו זעסט מיך אָפּקילן אין שנײַ אַ הײסן מעסער.

געדענק, אַז אויך דער וואָלקן איז פֿאַרזײַט מיט מײַן געבײן,
און רעגנט מיט מײַן אויפֿגעבליצטן פֿנים צו דער נידער.
פֿאַרזאַמל־מיך־צוזאַמען—איך זאָל קענען זײַן אַלײן,
אַלײן מיט דיר, און דו—אין מײַנע גלידער.

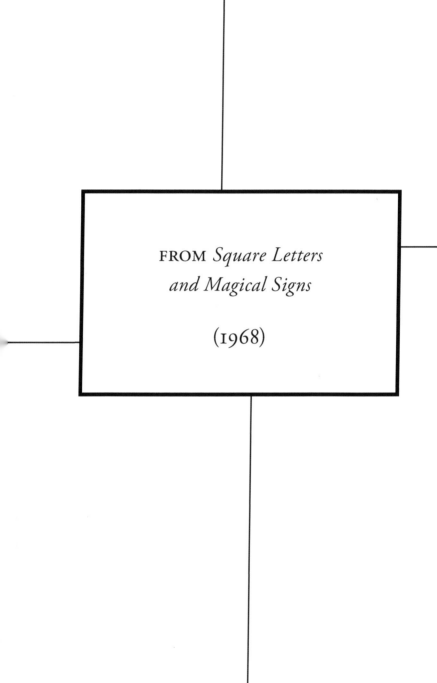

FROM *Square Letters
and Magical Signs*

(1968)

When the River Overran Its Banks

I was as old as the height of my knees now,
when the river overran its banks.
Then time itself knelt before me,
when the river overran its banks.

For my sake, a straw roof came swimming by,
with an eminent rooster on his straw throne,
his cock-a-doodle-doo, his whole manner—
as if he were a Gypsy.

Years later, when the disaster struck,
it suddenly become clear to me, like an axe in a dream,
that that roof is really all mine, all mine.

For my sake, an oak went swimming by, so nobly,
and wanted to shed its copper bark,
its molar-roots protruding as it floated along with the river.

Years later I saw it in Africa,
swimming quickly in the grass,
in the form of a lion pursuing a terrified doe.

ווען דער טײַך איז אַרויס פֿון די ברעגן

איך בין אַלט געווען דעמאָלט, ווי איצט ביז די קני,
ווען דער טײַך איז אַרויס פֿון די ברעגן.
נאָר די צײַט איז געשטאַנען פֿאַר מיר אויף די קני,
ווען דער טײַך איז אַרויס פֿון די ברעגן.

צוליב מיר איז געשוווומען אַ שטרוייענער דאַך,
מיט אַ האָן אויבן אָן אויפֿן שטרוייענעם טראָן,
און זײַן קוקעריקו און זײַן גאַנצער פֿאַסאָן—
עלעהיי אַ ציגײַנער.

יאָרן שפּעטער, ווען ס׳האָט מיך געטראָפֿן דער שלאַק,
איז געוואָרן מיר קלאָר, ווי אין חלום אַ האַק,
אַז דער דאַך איז גאָר מײַנער, איז מײַנער.

צוליב מיר איז געשוווומען אַ דעמב, ווי אַ שׂררה,
און זיך אויסטאָן געוואָלט פֿון זײַן קופֿערנער קאָרע.
האָט מיט באַקטיינער־וואָרצלען פֿאָרויס—מיטן טײַך זיך געלאָזן.

יאָרן שפּעטער—געזען אים אין אַפֿריקע שווימען געשווינד
צווישן גראָזן,
אין געשטאַלט פֿון אַ לײַב נאָך אַן איבערגעציטערטער הינד.

Only once was I really jealous:
a piano, as if shot down, was floating by,
Chopin on it, weeping, like pouring rain,
when the river overran its banks!

Years later I solved the secret, that the piano is sunset,
with a black bent wing escorted by an ice floe,
that it was really a coffin, my fate facing me—

Even back then I was lying in the coffin,
when the river overran its banks.

1966

נאָר געוואָען בין איך איינס אויף אַן אמת מקנא:
ס׳איז געשוווומען, ווי אונטערגעעשאָסן, אַ פֿיאַנע,
און אויף איר האָט געכליפּעט שאָפּען, ווי אַ רעגן,
ווען דער טייך איז אַרויס פֿון די ברעגן!

יאָרן שפּעטער באַנומען דעם סוד, אַז די פֿיאַנע אין שקיעה,
מיטן שוואַרצן געבויגענעם פֿליגל באַגלייט פֿון אַ קריע,
איז געוואָען גאָר אַן אָרון, מײַן גורל אַנטקעגן—

איך אַליין בין שוין דעמאָלט אין אָרון געלעגן,
ווען דער טייך איז אַרויס פֿון די ברעגן.

1966

103

To Leivick

1

I want to write to Leivick today.
It's been a long time since Leivick got a letter from me.
His address? Not dark abyss, not gravenstone,
I'd like it to be blue, just as Tel Aviv is blue.

Leivick alone—the name—is address, is wonder,
is he who had sworn for so long
to sing of the muteness of word, ascetic, set apart,
until he himself was struck down, in body and song.

And then like a bequest, distributed his muteness
to us, so it should protect the mouth
with sounds that bloom in desert-like caves,
in the middle of multitudinous, confused howls.

2

I was standing in a New York cemetery
by Leivick's snow-covered remains. And all around—
worshippers of Yiddish. Frozen swans.
And it seemed to me that New York is also mute.

צו לייוויקן

צו לייוויקן וויל איך היינט שרייבן. ס׳האָט לייוויק
שוין יאָרן פֿון מיר ניט באַקומען קיין בריוו.
זיין אַדרעס? ניט פֿינצטערער תּהום, ניט מצבֿיק,
כ׳וואָלט וועלן אַז בלוי, ווי ס׳איז בלוי תּל־אָבֿיבֿ.

נאָר לייוויק—דער נאָמען—איז אַדרעס, איז וווּנדער,
איז דער וואָס האָט שטומקייט פֿון וואָרט אַזוי לאַנג
באַשוווירן צו זינגען אַסקעטיש, באַזונדער,
ביז אויסגעשטומט האָט ער זיין גוף און געזאַנג.

און דעמאָלט בירושה געטאָן אונדז פֿאַרטיילן
זיין שטומקייט, זי זאָל אונדז באַשיצן דאָס מויל
מיט קלאַנגען וואָס בליִען אין מידברשע היילן,
אין מיטן המונישן, דולן געהויל.

איך בין אויף ניו־יאָרקער בית־עלמין געשטאַנען
ביי לייוויקס פֿאַרשניטן געביין. און אַרום—
די דאַוונערס פֿון יידיש. פֿאַרפֿרוירענע שוואַנען.
און ס׳האָט מיר געדאַכט, אַז ניו־יאָרק איז אויך שטום.

Death hides itself behind silver bars.
No movement on wheel or roller.
New York, like the Sambation on Sabbath, trembles
restless in its rest, with an iron river at its throat.

Instead of its walls—stone forests.
Paralyzed in the sky—the eagles of snow.
And it seemed to me that the poet gives a command
and forever—the uproar becomes mute.

3

Leivick told me of a childhood dream:
He saw the fiery sphere from which
the earth appeared. And long ago
it gave birth to him in fire of the first color.

And redress of the soul was a constant theme
possessing him, and the prayer of the poet became:
He should be destined to write a poem about this.
And won't this plea reach where it needs to go?

I want to write to Leivick today.
It's been a long time since Leivick got a letter from me.
His address? Not dark abyss, not gravestone,
I'd like it to be blue, just as Tel Aviv is blue.

1966

ס׳באַהאַלט זיך דער טויט הינטער זילבערנע שטאַבעס.
ניטאָ קיין באַוועגונג אין ראָד און אין וואַלץ.
און ס׳שלידדערט מיט רו, ווי סמבטיון אום שבת,
ניו־יאָרק, מיטן אײַזערנעם טײַך אױפֿן האַלדז.

אַנשטאָט אירע מויערן—שטײַנערנע וועלדער.
געליימטע אין הימל—די אָדלערס פֿון שניי.
און ס׳האָט מיר געדאַכט, אַז עס גיט אַ באַפֿעל דער
פֿאַעט און אױף אייביק ווערט שטום דאָס געשריי.

ג

דערציילט האָט מיר לייוויק אַ ייִנגלשן חלום:
די פֿיערקוויל האָט ער געזען, וואָס פֿון איר—
געוואָרן די ערד. און זי האָט שוין אַ מאָל אים
געבוירן אין פֿיער בײַם ערשטן קאָליר.

און שטענדיק אַ תיקון געמאָנט האָט די טעמע,
און דאָס איז די תפֿילה געווען פֿון פֿאַעט:
באַשערט זאָל אים זײַן וועגן דעם אַ פֿאָעמע.
צי וועט ניט דערגיין ווי עס דאַרף זײַן געבעט?

צו לייוויקן וויל איך הײַנט שרײַבן. ס׳האָט לייוויק
שױן יאָרן פֿון מיר ניט באַקומען קיין בריוו.
זײַן אַדרעס? ניט פֿינצטערער תהום, ניט מצבֿיק,
כ׳וואָלט וועלן אַז בלוי, ווי ס׳איז בלוי תל־אָבֿיבֿ.

1966

107

Poem without a Name

I drift to a gray region, and I'm pulled
downward to the dream-entrance. Under
my sleep I awake in the Bronx Zoo. The exits
clang shut, the slams of lock-up time
in prison movies. Walkways are deserted, kiosks
shuttered, the keeper gone with his keys.

A hand with stars on its fingers moves among
the branches and writes a large R and a large F
above the cages. All their doors fling open
and the animals rush out. They pass the low
barriers and move around me. I am the one
who is trapped now, who is gaped at.

With a hairy soul and a chest smooth and black
as a bed of coal, a gorilla hulks up and asks,
"Why are you trembling so? I'm also two-footed,
and I have a heart like yours. Look, we're not
so different. I only want to feed on your death.
I only want to feast on what we have in common."

ליד אָן אַ נאָמען

אַ חלום לאָזט מיך ניט אַנטרינען פֿון זײַן לאַנגן לויער
און ווערט פֿאַרוואַנדלט אין אַ חיות־גאָרטן, ווו דער טויער
פֿאַרהאַקט. פֿאַרשלאָסן. יאָ, אַוועק דער שומר און פֿאַרשלאָסן
אַזאַ מין חצות איז הימל ווײַט פֿון אַלע מײַנע חצותן:

אַ האַנט מיט שטערן אויף די פֿינגער ווײַזט זיך צווישן צווײַגן
און שרײַבט אַ גרויסן אַלף און אַ סמך איבער שטײַגן.
צעעפֿענען זיך שלעסער, און די חיות—נענטער, נענטער
צום איינציקן פֿאַרשלאָסענעם, צו מיר אַליין, דעם צענטער.

צו מיר, דעם ערד־געבונדענעם, וואָס פֿרײַ איז בלויז מײַן תּפֿילס,
דערנענטערט זיך מיט דער האָריקער נשמה אַ גאָרילע:
—וואָס ציטערסטו? צוווײַפֿיסיק איז מײַן האַרץ ווי דײַנס,
פֿאַרגלײַך עס—
צעקריען וויל איך בלויז דײַן טויט און ווײַסן אונדזער שײַכות.

אַ פֿעלדמאַרשאַל מיט אַ מאָנאָקל, טאָפּנדיק אַ מאָפּע—
אַזוי זעט אויס דער טיגער ווען עס צערטלט מיך זײַן לאַפּע:
—מיר האָבן זיך באַגעגנט בײַ אַ וואַסער אין ראָדעזיע,
אַצינד בין איך געקומען צו פֿאַרזוכן דײַן פּאָעזיע.

109

A field marshal wearing a monocle while his fingers
are tapping on a map, his swagger stick behind
his back—that's what the leopard looks like
as he strokes me with his paws. He reminds me,
"We once met at a waterhole in Zimbabwe, when you
were on safari. Now I've come to taste your poetry."

Like a young woman, showy, thriving, with wanton glances
while accompanying the coffin of her old husband—
a cobra covered in black. She hisses in my ear:
"We're both poison, and two doses of poison poison grief."

The hand with the stars on its fingers grows dim,
this poem a remnant of the zoo-dream.
Pray. If you still can pray.
The tiger and the snake and the gorilla caged again.

און ווי אַ יונגע פֿרוי מיט עולם־הזהדיקע בליקלעך,
באַגלייטנדיק איר אַלטנס אָרון, אויסגעפוצט און גליקלעך—
אַ קאָברעשלאַנג אין שוואַרצן קלייד. זי ציישעט מיר אין אויער:
—מיר זענען ביידע סם, און צוויי מאָל סם פֿאַרסמט דעם טרויער.

די האַנט מיט שטערן אויף די פֿינגער שוויימט אַוועק אַלץ בלייכער,
פֿון חלום וועגן חיות־גאַרטן איז דאָס ליד אַ זכר:
—בן־אָדם, טו אַ תּפֿילה וואָס דו קענסט נאָך טאָן אַ תּפֿילה.

────────

צוריק אין שטייג דער טיגער און די שלאַנג און די גאָרילע.

תּל־אָבֿיבֿ, 16טן פֿעברואַר 1967

III

FROM

Ripe Faces

(1970)

Portrait

Like Chaim Soutine's painting of hanging meat,
lit up with a golden, otherworldly grace—
that's how Max Brod appeared, darkling, the last time
I saw him in his old apartment on Jordan St.,
the name of his street which really was for him the Jordan.

The suspenders on his short-sleeve shirt
held him captive in the black chains of Galileo.
Yet, between them, his hunchback rose in glory,
like a monument of his own making.
And Prague and Kafka nuzzled along the walls.

And suddenly he stretched out his hands in blessing,
poked among books and pinched out a book
bound in snakeskin,
and read by heart a stanza by Hofmannsthal.

The ears of the kitten on the sofa tuned in.

פּאָרטרעט

ווי חיים סוטינס אַ געמעל פֿון העננגענדיקן פֿלייש,
באַלויכטן מיט אַ גילדענעם, יעננוועלטיקן גענאַד,
אַזוי האָט זיך אַנטפּלעקט פֿאַר מיר דאָס לעצטע מאָל מאַקס בראָד,
פֿאַרטונקלט אין זײַן אַלטער דירה אויף רחוֹב הירדן—
דער נאָמען פֿון זײַן גאַס, וואָס איז געוועזן פֿאַר אים דער ירדן.

די שלייקעס אויף זײַן העמד מיט קורצע אַרבל
געהאַאַלטן האָבן אים געפֿאַנגען אין די שוואַרצע קייטן
פֿון גאַליליי.
נאָר צווישן זיי דער הויקער אויפֿן פֿלייצע האָט מיט גלאָריע
געהויבן זיך, ווי זײַן אַליין געבויטער מאָנומענט.
און פֿראַג און קאַפֿקאַ האָבן זיך געלאַשטשעט אויף די ווענט.

און פּלוצעם האָט ער אויסגעצויגן בענטשנדיקע הענט,
געניסטערט צווישן ביכער און אַרויסגעקניפּט אַ בוך
אין שלאַנגענהויט געבונדן,
פֿון אים געלייענט אויסנווייניק האָפֿמאַנסטאַלס אַ סטראָפֿע.

ס׳האָט אָנגעסטרויעט אויערלעך דאָס קעצל אויף דער סאָפֿע.

And as he reads, a flood of tears suddenly pours out from
      him,
a spring rain from the clouds of his eyes
which become younger and bluer.
The words quicken to an awakening from dusty solitude,
from yellow sadness,
in his hands separated from Prague.

"I can't help myself—
for Heaven's sake—
that's how I greet beauty."

And the monument of his own making casts a shadow.

1969

און ווי ער לייענט, ערשט עס יאָגט פֿון אים א מחנה טרערן,
אַ פֿרילינג־רעגן פֿון די אויגן־וואָלקנדלעך וואָס ווערן
אַלץ יינגער, בלוייער.
די אויתיות גיבן אַ דערוואַך פֿון שטויביקער אַליינקייט,
פֿון געלן טרויער,
אין זײַנע פּראַגער אָפּגעשײַדטע הענט.

—איך קאָן ניט אַנדערש,
מענטשנקינד,
אַזוי באַגריס איך שײַנקייט———

און ס׳וואַרפֿט אַ שאָטן זײַן אַליין געבוירטער מאָנומענט.

1969

Firefighters

Firefighters attack me late at night,
like nimble acrobats
in a circus,
on long ladders
quickly shot up to me
on the sixth floor.

Firefighters.
Rivers on their shoulders.
Axes and helmets.
Ripping pieces of flesh from my innocent walls.
A mirror shatters. Repay me what you owe me: A bit of my face.
Crowbars.
Streams.
Pillars of the air totter.
Men stand below
holding an outspread net.
Screaming—
they're fainthearted—
I should take pity on them
and jump immediately.

פֿיער־לעשער

פֿיער־לעשער זענען מיך באַפֿאַלן שפּעט בײַ נאַכט,
ווי ספּריטנע אַקראָבאַטן
אין אַ צירק,
אויף לאַנגע לײַטערס,
געשווינד אַרויפֿגעשאַסענע צו מיר
צום זעקסטן גאָרן.

פֿיערלעשער.
טײכן אויף די אַקסלען.
העק און העלמען.
רײַסן שטיקער פֿלייש פֿון מײַנע אומשולדיקע ווענט.
ס׳פּלאַצט אַ שפּיגל. צאַלט מיר אָפּ אַ חובֿ: אַ שטיקל פנים.
לאָמען.
שטראָמען.
ס׳וואַקלען זיך די זײַלן פֿון דער לופֿט.
אונטן שטייען מענטשן
מיט אַן אויסגעשפּרייטער נעץ.
ליאַרעמען,
—זיי האָבן שוואַכע הערצער—
איך זאָל זיך גליבך דערבאַרעמען
און שפּרינגגען.

And I,
on the sixth floor,
in a royal pose,
am immersed in the work of a poet from the 13th century,
astonished
that the firefighters
attack me at night
with axes and helmets and insolence,
burning with zeal not to let me burn.

1970

און איך, אויף זעקסטן גאָרן,

אין אַ קעניגלעכער פּאָזע,

לייען גאָר אַ דיכטער פֿונעם דרײַצעטן יאָרהונדערט

און בין פֿאַרוווּנדערט,

אַלמאַי די פֿיִער־לעשער זעגנען

באַפֿאַלן מיך בײַ נאַכט

מיט העק און העלמען און מיט העזה,

און מיט אַ ברען זיי לאָזן מיך ניט ברענען.

1970

FROM

The Fiddle Rose

(1974)

Granite Wings

The cold granite wings
sunk in the earth,
bound with earth-chains
to the body below—
the only witnesses
that he is still here.
The witnesses to his past experience, → buried books
other creatures,
crave newly made words:
they're usually buried
outside the cemetery.

The cold granite wings   marker sinks in to get body
sunk in the earth
draw closer to the body below.
They feel his non-death:
a bony pair of pliers → tongs
and a soul crushed between the pincers.

* Also books living

124

גראַניטענע פֿליגל

די קאַלטע גראַניטענע פֿליגל
פֿאַרזונקען אין ערד,
געבונדן מיט ערדענע קייטן
צום גוף אין דער נידער
זענען די איינציקע עדות
אַז ער איז נאָך דאָ.
די עדות אַז ער איז געווען
זענען אַנדערע ברואים,
און ס׳בעט זיך אַ נעאָלאָגיזם:
זיי זענען געוועגעלעך
מחוץ דעם בית־עלמין.

די קאַלטע גראַניטענע פֿליגל
פֿאַרזונקען אין ערד,
ציִען זיך נעגטער צום גוף אין דער נידער.
זיי פֿילן
זײן אומטויט:
אַ ביינערנע צוואַנג
און אין צוואַנג איז פֿאַרדרייקט אַ נשמה.

125

The cold granite wings
start to shiver
as a sun shower soaks them through and through,
streaming into their veins.
A back-from-the-dead song of spring.
They wrench
themselves loose
from the stony earth, from the earth-chains,
along with the body coated dusty green. *mold / death*

Where are they flying off to? → *redemption*
If I knew where—
I would go on foot with them, *taking a body*
go with them *out of ground*
in my dream of them, → *thru life / for ...*
along with the body coated dusty green. *mold / dead*

1972

4 redemption
↓
Heaven and
moving thrum
to a better
place

ס׳דערלאַנגען אַ ציטער

די קאַלטע גראַניטענע פֿליגל:

אַ זונרעגן ווייקט זיי אַדורך,

שטראָמט אַרײַן אין די אָדערן.

אַ תּחית־המתים־געזאַנג פֿון אַ פֿרילינג.

זיי רײַסן

זיך אָפּ

פֿון דער פֿעלדזיקער ערד, פֿון די ערדענע קײטן,

בײַנאַנד מיטן גוף אין אַ מאַנטל פֿון שטױביקן גרין.

ווּהין זייער פֿליעניש? אַז איך וואָלט וויסן ווּהין—

איך וואָלט זיי צו פֿוס און צו חלום באַגלייטן, באַגלייטן.

1972

From Both Ends of the World

I

From both ends of the world
we stare and shudder:
two mirrors blue from cold,
and harbor against harbor.

Just a little match,
strike it—and teardrop
will madly fall
in love with teardrop.

With this spark
everything will fall apart,
just as in one second
circus tents collapse.

But you're too in love
with your love to strike
the match: it's over,
everthing's now over.

I myself choke my tongue
from envy, in case
it tells of my happiness,
now over. You are gone.

פֿון ביידע עקן וועלט

פֿון ביידע עקן וועלט
מיר שוידערן און גאַפֿן:
צוויי שפּיגלען בלוי פֿון קעלט
און האַפֿן קעגן האַפֿן.

אַ שוועבעלע, ניט מער,
געגוג דו זאָלסט אַ ריב טאָן—
און ס'וועט זיך טרער־אין־טרער
משוגע אַ פֿאַרליב טאָן.

צעפֿאַלן זיך ביים צונד
וועט אַלצדינג מיט אַנאַנדער.
אַזוי אין איין סעקונד
אַ צירק עס פֿאַלט פֿונאַנדער.

נאָר צו פֿיל האָסטו ליב
דײַן ליבשאַפֿט, זאָלסט דערלאָנגען
די שוועבעלע אַ ריב,
און אויס. און אַלץ פֿאַרגאַנגען.

און איך אַליין דערשטיק
מײַן צונג פֿון קינאה, טאָמער
דערצייילט זי פֿון מײַן גליק,
און אויס. דו ביסט ניטאָ מער.

From both ends of the world,
one God shaped us:
two mirrors blue from cold,
and harbor against harbor.

2

Don't be late. Too bad. For a few seconds
the ocean recedes, giving you a chance to find
its treasure ashore, the tufts of spume
like morning stars in the blue dawn.

Run alongside the teeth of the wave.
The treasure cries from joy. There's no . . . soon.
Reach into the wave's joy-lament; otherwise,
it will be swallowed up by its own folds.

Just once, this temptation meant for you,
for just a few seconds, the ocean edge stark naked,
the treasure of the ocean confided only to you,
the pearl of its heart a still small voice.

A ship sinks, leaving only some drops of oil.
You're late. The trace won't remain long.
Late? No, even death may bless survival.
You already hold the treasure. Hymn it.

1971

פֿון ביידע עקן וועלט
איין גאָט האָט אונדז באַשאַפֿן:
צוויי שפּיגלען בלוי פֿון קעלט
און האָפֿן קעגן האָפֿן.

ב

פֿאַרשפּעטיק ניט. אַ שאָד. געצײלטע רגעס
טרעט אָפּ דער ים צוריק, דו זאָלסט געפֿינען
זײַן אוֹצר אויף די אָפּגעשוימטע ברעגעס,
ווי מאָרגן־שטערן אינעם בלוי־באַגינען.

פֿאַרלויף אַנטקעגן ים די צײן פֿון כוואַליע.
דער אוֹצר וויינט פֿון פֿרייד. ניטאָ קיין באַלדן.
דערלאַנג זיך אויף זײַן פֿריידגעוויין אַ וואַליע,
אַניט פֿאַרשלינגט זי אים אין אירע פֿאַלדן.

איינמאָליק איז באַשערט אַזאַ נסיון,
געצײלטע רגעס איז דער ים־זוים נאַקעט.
זײַן אוֹצר וויל דער ים בלויז **דיר** געטרויען,
דער פּערל פֿון זײַן הארץ קול־דממה־דקהט.

אַ שיף גייט אונטער בליבט אַ טראָפּן ווימל,
פֿאַרשפּעטיקסטו—ניט בלײַבן וועט קיין סימן.
פֿאַרשפּעטיקט? ניין, דער טויט מעג באַענטשן גומל:
דו האָסט אים שוין דעם אוֹצר. זינג אַ הימען.

1971

The Full Pomegranate

I

The pomegranate, full, full with lightning and dark clouds,
compressed and armored.
You don't see its frightening appearance,
don't drink its lightning and dark clouds, sister.

Lava—its grains. Genesis—
atoms turbulent, bursting
even before the fruit had a name:
just now the world breaking from its chambers.

The pomegranate, full—youth is in its oldness,
oldness is in its youth. It holds both
inward in its full root cellar—
death and life unwilling to separate.

The pomegranate, full, drunk from wine
millions of years old. You won't be able
to bend over it as over a well:
armored on the outside and you don't see it.

פֿול דער מילגרוים

פֿול דער מילגרוים. פֿול מיט בלִיץ און כמאַרע,
פֿאַנצערדיק אין דרויסן אַ פֿאַרפרעסטער.
זעסטו ניט זײַן מוראדיקע מראה,
טרינקסטו ניט זײַן בלִיץ און כמאַרע, שוועסטער.

לאָוע זײַנע קערנדלעך. אַטאָמען
בראשיתדיק אַרויסגעוויירטע, איידער
ס׳האָט די פֿרי נאָך געהאַט אַ נאָמען:
אָקערשט איז נאָך וועלט אַרויס פֿון חדר.

פֿול דער מילגרוים. יונג איז אים זײַן עלטער,
אַלט איז אים זײַן יונגשאַפֿט. ער האָט בײידן
אינעוויינִיק אין זײַן פֿולן קעלטער—
טויט און לעבן וויל זיך ניט צעשיידן.

פֿול דער מילגרוים. שיכור איז ער פֿונעם
ווײַן מיליאָנען־יאָריקן. דו וועסט ניט
בײַגן זיך פֿאַר אים ווי פֿאַר אַ ברונעם:
דרויסן איז אַ פֿאַנצער און דו זעסט ניט.

2

And wherever you wander
and wherever you live,
you wander around a pomegranate, sister,
live in my pomegranate arch,
radiant and sliced open.

Even before you were born
you already read somewhere
in the cosmic classifieds:
Room for Rent.

My street is longer than a light year,
with no lack of rooms on both sides
and nets over the thresholds.
You moved into what loved you:
to live in my pomegranate arch,
radiant and sliced open.

Granite on my eyelashes.
Green eternity of earth.
And you, my spring dancer,
you dance further,
drunk in my pomegranate arch,
delighting a young boy.

ב

און וווּ דו זאָלסט ניט וואַנדערן
און וווּ דו זאָלסט ניט וויינען,
וואַנדערסטו אַרום אַ מילגרוים, שוועסטער,
וווינסטו אין מײַן מילגרוימשלײף
דעם זוניק אויפֿגעשניטענעם.

נאָך איידער ביסט געבוירן
האָסטו ערגעץ שוין געלייענט
אַ קאָסמישן אַנאָנס:
פֿאַראַן אַ צימער צו פֿאַרדינגען.

מײַן גאַס איז לענגער פֿון אַ ליכטיאָר,
ס׳פֿעלן ניט אין איר
פֿון ביידע זײַטן צימערן
מיט נעצן אויף די שוועלן.
אַרײַנגעקליבן האָסטו זיך
אין דעם וואָס האָט דיך ליב:
צו וווינען אין מײַן מילגרוימשלײף
דעם זוניק אויפֿגעשניטענעם.

גראַניט אויף מײַנע ווײַס.
גרינע אייביקייט פֿון ערד.
און דו, מײַן פֿרילינג־טענצערין,
טאַנצסט ווײַטער
פֿאַרשיכּורט אין מײַן מילגרוימשלײף,
אַ יינגל צו דערפֿרייען.

135

3

People will see dawn and shrug their shoulders:
rescued lips are pressed to mine.
Unimagined by anyone since people have had lips—
a holiday-fright, a wonder without a mask.

Doves will coo even more on my windowsills:
Besides my two lips, my lips will inherit two more.
My mouth will be sealed and locked
with small kissed lips closer to me than my own.

This wonder without a mask will last until evening,
the sun itself a witness, a trustworthy witness.
And if a shadow denies it all, the sun will grab him by his
        forelock
and drag him to the ocean and burn him and drown him.

Then a rain will run wild down from a cloudmountain
and with lightning in its belt overtake its sacrificial victim
and with a blessing—once, twice, more—cut up my lips.
The pieces and the raindrops will be mixed in together.

באגינען וועלן מענטשן זען און הייבן מיט די אקסלען:
גאראטעוועטע ליפן זענען צוגעקושט צו מײנע.
אזוינס געדענקט ניט קיינער זינט עס האבן מענטשן ליפן,
ס'וועט זײן א יום־טובֿדיקע שרעק, א וווּנדער אן א מאסקע.

עס וועלן עקסטרע וואָרקען אויף מײן פֿענצטערגזימס די טויבן:
אהין די אייגענע צוויי ליפן האָט ער אויך געירשנט
צוויי אַנדערע. מײן מויל וועט זײן פֿאַרזיגלט און פֿאַרשלאָסן
מיט קלײנע צוגעקושטע ליפן אייגענער ווי מײנע.

דער וווּנדער אן א מאסקע וועט געדויערן ביז אָוונט,
אַליין די זון זאָל זײן אן עדות, א באַגלייבטער עדות.
און וועט א שאָטן לייקענען—זי וועט אים פֿאַר די לאָקן
אַרײנשלעפֿן אין ים און אי פֿאַרברענען, אי דערטרינקען.

און דעמאָלט וועט אראָפֿריטן פֿון וואָלקנבאַרג א רעגן,
צוזאַמען מיט א בליץ אין גאָרטל אָניאָגן זײן קרבן
און מיט א ברכה—מײנע ליפן, צוויי מאָל צוויי, צעשנידן.
צוזאַמענמישן וועלן זיך די טיילן און די טראָפֿנס.

137

4

We both eat fire from the same fork,
a bit of fire that's called happiness.
Why is the fright between us doubled
and the river between us without a bridge?

Why is the earth full of caves, crevices
and craters where there's no living thing
and there is no place where
fewer than three human beings can hide?

No one can even laugh without another,
laughter slammed shut behind a lock.
Why can no one accompany them both
except the jealous mind? Why?

מיר עסן ביידע פֿונעם זעלבן גאָפּל

אַ שטיקל פֿיער וואָס מע רופֿט עס גליק.

פֿאַר וואָס איז אויך די שרעק ביי ביידן טאָפּל

און צווישן אונדז דער טייך איז אָן אַ בריק?

פֿאַר וואָס איז פֿול די ערד מיט היילן, שפּאַלטן

און קראַטערס וווּ עס וווינט ניט קיין בעל־חי

און ס'איז ניטאָ קיין אָרט זיך צו באַהאַלטן

פֿאַר מענטשנקינדער וווינציקער ווי דריי?

ס'קאָן איינער דאָך ניט לאַכן אָנעם צווייטן,

פֿאַרהאַקט איז דאָס געלעכטער אויף אַ שלאָס.

פֿאַר וואָס קאָן ביידן קיינער ניט באַגלייטן

אַהין די קינאה פֿונעם גייסט? פֿאַר וואָס?

5

The same? No, my faces wander around, lost,
and I myself cannot recognize them anymore:
flamyhaired, snoweyed and rutted,
raveled like wild geese and mortal.
Disembodied—they hear, are vulnerable,
hidden, see but are not seen.
Although an individual creature draws them along,
this amazing encounter is nearby:
a night of blue heads in pyramids,
a desert sand of burned-out tribes.

And there, sister, I bless the land of peace
and lay my last breath at your feet.

1971–1972

דער זעלבער? נייַן, עס בלאַנדזשען מײַנע פֿנימער
און איך אַליין קאָן אויך זיי ניט דערקענען מער:
פֿלאַמהאַריקע, שנייאויגיקע און קאַרביקע,
צעשויבערטע ווי ווילדע גענדז און שטאַרביקע.
אַנגופֿיקע—זיי הערן, זענען שפֿירעוודיק,
פֿאַרהוילענע און רואה־ואינו־ניראהדיק.
און ווײַל זיי ציט אַן איינציקע באַשעפֿעניש,
איז נאָענט שוין די ווונדערלעכע טרעפֿעניש:
אַ נאַכט פֿון בלויע קעפ אין פֿיראַמידן,
אַ מידבר־זאַמד פֿון אויסגעברענטע שבֿטים.

און דאָרטן, שוועסטער, בענטש איך ס'לאַנד פֿון פֿרידן
און לייג צו דײַנע פֿיס מײַן לעצטן אָטעם.

1971–1972

Collected Treasures

I have collected treasures and secreted them in safes,
and no one besides me knows the combination.
And now, I say—my throbbing temples as witness:
"Time to go back home, back to basics, get rid of the
     management."

Let a river impulsively swim out of the word-bed "river"
together with a girl on a coverlet of red plush,
and let her live in reality, in real live fantasy,
and let the diamond of her kiss cut to the bone.

Let the word "birch" go back to being a tree in the forest, birch,
let each and every image go back to its original design.
Let "The red cow of sunset" return to being prose
and "Food for the soul"—become snow, not food.

Back home, back to basics, my dreams, images,
I free lightning from its cage so it shows what it can do.
And when the calm and clamor subside—let
a wet rooster announce the good tidings throughout the
     world.

1972

געזאַמלט אוצרות

געזאַמלט האָב איך אוצרות און פֿאַרסודעט זיי אין סײַפֿן,
חוץ מיר האָט קיינער ניט געוווּסט ווי עפֿענען דעם שלאָס.
און איצטער זאָג איך, עדות מײַנע קלאָפֿעדיקע שלייפֿן:
—צוריק אַהיים, צום עלעמענט, און אויס מיט בעל־הבית.

אַרויסשווימען פֿון וואָרט־געלעגער ,,טיך''—אַ טײַך זאָל האָסטיק
צוזאַמען מיטן מיידל אױפֿן דעק פֿון ראָזן פֿליוש,
און זאָל זי לעבן אויף דער וואָר, אין וואָריקער פֿאַנטאַסטיק,
און זאָל צעשנײַדן בײַן דער דימענט פֿון איר קוש.

צוריק זאָל ס'וואָרט ,,בעריאָזע'' ווערן בוים אין וואַלד, בעריאָזע,
צוריק זאָל זיך פֿאַרוואַנדלען יעדער בילד אין זײַן מאָדעל.
,,די רויטע קו פֿון זונפֿאַרגאַנג'' זאָל ווידער ווערן פֿראָזע
און ,,מעל פֿאַר דער נשמה''—ווערן שנײַ, ניטאָ קיין מעל.

צוריק אַהיים, צום עלעמענט, חלומות מײַנע, בילדער,
כ'באַפֿרײַ פֿון שטעג אַ בליץ און זאָל ער ווײַזן וואָס ער קאָן.
און ווען עס וועט זיך אײַנשטילן די רו און דאָס געפֿילדער—
זאָל אָנזאָגן די בשׂורה גאָר דער וועלט אַ נאַסער האָן.

1972

Wonder

(for Dov Sadan)

This too can happen, without harm,
whether it's wonder or romanticism:
a young silence knocks on a shutter,
and the night in the room is four-sided.

If that is wonder—the reality on both
sides of the shutter is also wonder.
I know, my reality is more than wonder,
I know, my dream is well-grounded:

I saw clearly in a dream
a real cherry tree, loaded with cherries,
close at hand, and—farther away . . .
clearly, the tree was rooted in the ground.

And if that's too little and not enough—
when I awake at dawn
I devour the cherries—tongue and teeth—
by the cherry-red of the drapes.

In order to convince myself
that dream lives in peace with reality—
I swing the branches in reality,
that have sprouted from dream.

June 8, 1972

וווּנדער

(פֿאַר דבֿ סדן)

אַזוינס קאַן אויך געשען, אָן שאָדן.
זאָל זײַן ס׳איז וווּנדער צי ראָמאַנטיק:
אַ יונגע שטילקייט קלאַפֿט אין לאָדן,
די נאַכט אין צימער איז פֿירקאַנטיק.

אוי **דאָס** איז וווּנדער—איז אויך וווּנדער
די וואָר פֿון ביידע זײַטן לאָדן.
איך וווייס, מײַן וואָר איז מער ווי וווּנדער,
איך וווייס, מײַן חלום האָט אַ באָדן:

געזען אין חלום האָב איך דײַטלעך
אַ וואָרן קאַרשנבוים, באַלאָדן
מיט קאַרשן האַנטיק־נאָנט און—וווּיטלעך . . .
איז קלאָר, דער בוים איז פֿאַרמאָגט אַ באָדן.

און אויב ס׳איז וווינציק, אויב ס׳איז ווייניק—
אַצינד, בײַם אויפֿוואַכן באַגינען,
איך שלינג די קאַרשן צונגיק־צייניק
בײַם קאַרשנרויט פֿון די גאַרדינען.

כּדי איך זאָל זיך איבערצײַגן
ווי חלום לעבט מיט וואָר בשלום—
צעוויג איך אויף דער וואָר די צווײַגן,
ארויסגעוואָקסענע פֿון חלום.

8טן יוני 1972

Alto Cellos

No, we both won't end,
our beginning still near, intimate.
We'll only end the way between us
and set free a new vista.

Both of us will meet again
in a mirror: Behind it alto cellos
will rain on the grass
and the mirror won't be made of glass.

Not of glass but of a weaving
thoroughly familiar and tangible:
Behind it a new experience,
and death will hang by a hair.

Is it possible that we are mistakes,
accidental our beautiful hour,
and a blind worm will eat up that hour,
only clay shards left at the bitter end?

No, we will both meet
like destined sounds in a stanza.
Alto cellos will rain
over white forests of infinity.

1972

הויכע וויאָלאָנטשעלן

נ‏יין, מיר וועלן ביידע זיך ניט ענדיקן,
אונדזער אָנהייב איז נאָך היימיש‏־נאָענט.
מיר'ן בלויז דעם לויז גאַנג צו זיך פֿאַרענדיקן
און ס'איז פֿרי אַ נײַער האָריזאָנט.

ביידע וועלן ווידער זיך באַגעגענען
אין אַ שפּיגל: הינטער אים אין גראַז
וועלן הויכע וויאָלאָנטשעלן רעגענען
און דער שפּיגל וועט ניט זײַן פֿון גלאָז.

ניט פֿון גלאָז נאָר פֿון אַזאַ מין וועבעניש
קענטלעך און ממשותדיק ביז גאָר:
הינטער אים—אַ נײַע איבערלעבעניש,
און דער טויט וועט הענגען אויף אַ האָר.

איז דען מעגלעך אַז מיר זענען טעותן,
צופֿעליק איז אונדזער שענסטע שעה
און אַ בלינדער וואָרעם זאָל די שעה עסן,
בלײַבן זאָלן שערבלעך אויפֿן דנאָ?

נ‏יין, מיר וועלן ביידע זיך באַגעגענען
ווי באַשערטע קלאַנגען אין אַ סטראָף.
הויכע וויאָלאָנטשעלן וועלן רעגענען
איבער ווײַסע וועלדער פֿון אין‏־סוף.

1972

147

Here I am fated to see silence through a tear,
blooming as it can from humidity and prosperity.
Eye to eye with silence and hearing to hearing—
my destiny is to breathe its gleaming thought.

Childhood odor. Beginning of my beginning, of my descent,
eagle-shadow whets its black knife on the cliffs.
Fire spurts in a wadi, first snow its savor:
as a child on a mountain, I had such a revelation.

Child on a mountain three thousand years ago?
Years are drops in water, too many to count.
Once I left my gaze in the weft of sun,
and once wrote down a line with a piece of chalk.

Now I want to drink up the whole morning,
even light not enough for me to fledge a new line.
Someone wants my soul to fall to its knees
before it rises brand new in humid mirrors.

1971

דאָ איז מיר באַשערט צו זען די שטילקייט דורך אַ טרער,
בליען זאָל זי קאָנען פֿון דער פֿליכטיקייט און געדיען.
אויג אויף אויג מיט שטילקייט און געהער צו איר געהער—
אָטעמען איז מיר באַשערט איר גליענדיקן רעיון.

קינדהייט־ריח. אַנהייב פֿון מײַן אָנהייב, פֿון מײַן שטאַם.
אַדלער־שאָטן שליטפֿט זײַן שװאַרצן מעסער אָן די סקאַלעס.
פֿיער שפּרודלט אין אַ װאָדי, ערשטער שנײַ זײַן טעם,
קינדװײַז אויף אַ באַרג האָב איך געהאַט אַזאַ התגלות.

קינדװײַז אויף אַ באַרג מיט יאָרן דרײַ טויזנט צוריק?
יאָרן זענען טראָפּנס אין אַ װאַסער, צייל ניט װיפֿל.
כ׳האָב געלאָזן דאָ אַ מאָל אין זונגעװעב מײַן בליק,
כ׳האָב פֿאַרשריבן דאָ אַ מאָל אַ שורה מיט אַ גריפֿל.

איצטער װיל איך אויסטרינקען דעם גאַנצן אינדערפֿרי,
װינציק איז מיר ליכט אַ נײַע שורה צו באַפֿליגלען.
עמעץ װיל ס׳זאָל פֿאַלן מײַן נשמה אויף די קני
איידער זי װעט אויפֿגיין שפּאָגל נײַ אין פֿײַכטע שפּיגלען.

1971

149

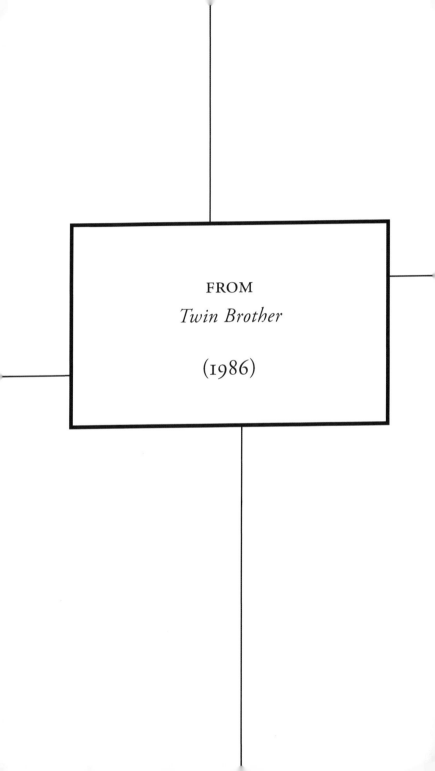

FROM

Twin Brother

(1986)

1974

Who will last, what will last? A wind will last.
The blind will die, their blindness last.
The ocean's raveled foam will last.
A cloud snagged by a tree will last.

Who will last, what will last? A syllable will last,
as Creation seeds again and lasts.
For its own sake, a fiddle rose will last.
Seven blades of grass that know the rose will last.

Longer than all the northern stars will last,
the star that falls in a tear will last.
In the jug, a drop of wine will last.
Who will last, what will last? God will last.

Isn't that enough for you?

ווער וועט בליבן, וואָס וועט בליבן? בלייבן וועט אַ ווינט,
בלייבן וועט די בלינדקייט פֿונעם בלינדן וואָס פֿאַרשווינדט.
בלייבן וועט אַ סימן פֿונעם ים: אַ שנירל שוים,
בלייבן וועט אַ וואָלקנדל פֿאַרטשעפּעט אויף אַ בוים.

ווער וועט בלייבן, וואָס וועט בלייבן? בלייבן וועט אַ טראַף,
בראשיתדיק אַרויסצוגראָזן ווידער זײַן באַשאַף.
בלייבן וועט אַ פֿידלרויז לכּבֿוד זיך אַליין,
זיבן גראָזן פֿון די גראָזן וועלן זי פֿאַרשטיין.

מער פֿון אַלע שטערן אַזש פֿון צפֿון ביז אַהער,
בלייבן וועט דער שטערן וואָס ער פֿאַלט אין סאַמע טרער.
שטענדיק וועט אַ טראָפּן ווײַן אויך בלייבן אין זײַן קרוג.
ווער וועט בלייבן, גאָט וועט בלייבן, איז דיר ניט גענוג?

Good morning, woodpecker, if God forbid, you have nothing
    to peck,
glide over here and peck out my so-called power of reasoning,
what people consider the pick of the crop,
though according to my reckoning it's worth half a smile.

Glide over here to me my beaked one and anoint me as your
    fool;
indulge me in the bliss of your tooth-edged beak.
My days are symbols, built out of dream-clay,
but I will welcome you with bread and salt and garlic.

So many little angels of death spend time in my bark,
and each with its time-tested poison and bow and arrow.
They lie in wait. They are always living, real,
the kind that certainly penetrated both of Dante's eyes.

Glide over to me and peck out that power, do it skillfully—
I still have to be transformed into a child of six or seven,
I still have to demolish the powerful empire of words,
I still have to generate others, so I can love in other ways.

גוט־מאָרגן, פיקהאָלץ, אויב חלילה האָסט ניט וואָס צו פיקן,
דערשװעב אַהער און פיק מיר אויס, מישטיינס געזאָגט, מײן שׂכל
וואָס מענטשנקינדער מיינען: אַן אַרטיקל פֿון אַנטיקן,
און וועדליק מײן השׂגה איז ער וװערט אַ האַלבן שמייכל.

דערשוועב צו מיר, באַשנאָבלטער, און זאַלב מיך פֿאַר דײן שוטה,
פֿאַרגין מיר די מתיקות פֿון דײן ציינדלדיקן שנאָבל.
סימבאָלן זענען מײנע טעג, פֿון חלום־ליים געבריטע,
נאָר איכ׳ל דיך באַגעגענען מיט ברוויט און זאַלץ און קנאָבל.

אַזוי פֿיל מלאך־המוותלעך פֿאַרברענגען אין מײן קאָרע,
און יעדער מיט זײן אויסגעפֿרוװעטן סם און פֿײל־און־בויגן.
זײ לאָקערן. זײ זענען תּמיד לעבעדיקע, וואָרע,
אַזאַ האָט זיכער דורכגעשאָסן דאַנטען ביידע אויגן.

דערשוועב צו מיר און פיק זײ אויס דעם כּוח, זײ אַ בריה,
איך דאַרף זיך נאָך פֿאַרװאַאַנדלען אין אַ קינד פֿון זעקס צי זיבן,
איך דאַרף צעטרײסלען וװערטער, זײער מאַכטיקע אימפּעריע,
איך דאַרף באַשאַפֿן אַנדערע, צו קאָנען אַנדערש ליבן.

Fate—hairy dog—may your teeth live!
Tear apart, rip apart—just don't show me your servile paw.
Without wounds I am nothing. No one. Less than no one.
I would rather be a battlefield and a mysterious map.

The map is studded with pins, too many defeats to count,
and far off in the horizon my property burns in the rain.
Hairy dog, only your teeth can heal,
like herbs that sweeten the more they are bitter.

The pins skip around in my flesh from evening to dawn
and announce that somewhere my enemy prepares an elegy.
Hairy dog, I still have one defeat to win,
and now I trust seven drops of gold for my strategy.

All seven make a prism of my face. Each drop
rolled down with good luck, yet right away rolled backwards.
From my feet to my head, I love the white teeth of dread—
Tear apart, rip apart, only don't kiss the soles of my feet with
        regret . . .

קודלאַטער כלב—גורל, זאָלן לעבן דײַנע צײַנער!
צערײַס, צעפליק, נאָר ווײַז מיר ניט הכנעהדיק די לאַפע.
אָן וווּנדן בין איך גאָרנישט. קיינער. ווינציקער ווי קיינער.
כ׳וויל בעסער זײַן אַ שלאַכטפעלד און אַ סודותדיקע מאַפע.

באַשפילקעט איז די מאַפע מיט מפלות ניט צום צײַלן
און ווײַט בײַם האָריזאָנט אין רעגן ברענען מײַנע גיטער.
קודלאַטער כלב, בלויז די צײַנער דײַנע קאָנען היילן,
ווי קריטעכצער וואָס מאַכן זיס וואָס מער זיי זענען ביטער.

די שפילקעס היפערן אין לײַב פון אָוונט ביז באַגינען
און זאָגן אָן, אַז ערגעץ גרייט מײַן שׂונא אָן עלעגיע.
קודלאַטער כלב, כ׳האָב נאָך אײַן מפלה צו געווינען,
און זיבן טראָפּנס גאָלד פֿאַרטרוי איך איצטער מײַן סטראַטעגיע.

אין אַלע זיבן פריזמעט זיך מײַן פנים. יעדער טראָפּן,
אַרויסגעקײַקלט זיך מיט מזל, בלײַבט שוין אַ קאָפּויער.
כ׳האָב ליב די ווײַסע צײַן פון שרעק צופוסן און צוקאָפּן,
צערײַס, צעפליק, נאָר קוש ניט מײַנע פיאַטעס מיט באַדויער . . .

Who blessed me has also cursed me.
I embrace in love the twinning of honey and of vinegar.
Thank you for blessing me with friends. Without their
        strength
my work along with me would fade by day and by night.

For my sake they paint and hammer and mold,
for my sake they roll down poems from their hearts.
Oh, my I's are they, those painters and poets,
and their I am I, even when I don't know whose.

For their sake I once sung in a coffin,
for their sake I still wage war over a comma,
and when they die, only then are my friends born
in the green cradle of my swaying soul.

For my sake they warm up the cold stars,
for my sake they play: a violin or a cello
brings forth from itself a joyous gush of my tears.
For their sake I write these very lines. Amen. Selah.

דער זעלביקער וואָס האָט גערבענטשט, ער האָט מיך אויך געשאָלטן.
כ׳נעם אָן פֿאַר ליב די צווילינגשאַפֿט פֿון האָניק און פֿון עסיק.
אַ דאַנק פֿאַר בענטשן מיך מיט פֿריינד. אָן זייער כּוח וואָלטן
ביינאַנד מיט מיר די ווערטער מיינע אויסגעצאַנקט מעת־לעתיק.

פֿאַר מײַנעט וועגן מאָלן זיי און האָמערן און קנעטן,
פֿאַר מײַנעט וועגן קײקלען זיי אַראָפֿ פֿון האַרץ פֿאַמעס.
אַ, מײַנע איכן זענען זיי, די מאָלערס און פֿאַעטן,
און זייער איך בין איך, אַפֿילו אַז איך וייס ניט וועמעס.

פֿאַר זייערט וועגן האָב איך וואָן געזונגען אין אַן אָרון,
פֿאַר זייערט וועגן האַלט איך נאָך מלחמה פֿאַר אַ קאַמע.
און שטאַרבן זיי, ערשט יעמאָלט ווערן מיינע פֿריינד געבאָרן
אין גרינער קינדערוויג פֿון מײַן צעהויעדעטער נשמה.

פֿאַר מײַנעט וועגן וואַרעמען זיי אָן די קאַלטע שטערן,
פֿאַר מײַנעט וועגן שפֿילן זיי: אַ פֿידל צי אַ טשעלאָ
דערלאַנגט פֿון זיך אַ קוואַל אַרויס מיט שׂימחה מײַנע טרערן.
פֿאַר זייערט וועגן שרייב איך די אַ שורות. אָמן־סלה.

1975–1976

Gone, the green pair of eyes of long, long ago. Their green
like an evergreen forest. As soon as I see those eyes, it is a sign
that they see me. And fir-branch-green is also my jealousy
of famished spirits, of sounds and of voices.

If God had only created their green that dark green
He would still be the same God. How could they
        not-become?
I wander in a forest: The sun burns in cobwebs,
green tears from green caves rustle among roots.

If this green pair of eyes would disappear forever,
instead of a forever there would be worm-eaten seconds.
I wander in a forest: It is night. A root still sprouts faithfully,
the sun in the cobwebs has not yet disappeared.

They see me, those dark-greens, waiting for a sign,
they tremble together, face to face with me.
And rustling tears from the green caves
swim into my vision and leave their glow to me.

ניטאָ די גרינע אויגנפּאָר פֿון לאַנג־לאַנג־לאַנג. די גרינע
ווי יאָדלעוואַלד. נאָר קוים איך זע די אויגן, איז אַ סימן:
זיי זעען מיך. און יאָדלע־צווייגן־גרין איז אויך מײַן קינאה
צו גיסטער אויסגעהונגערטע, צו קלאַנגען און צו שטימען.

ווען גאָט וואָלט בלויז באַשאַפֿן זייער גרין דאָס טונקל גרינע,
ער וואָלט געוועון דער זעלבער גאָט. ווי קאָנען זיי ניט־ווערן?
איך בלאָנדזשע אין אַ וואַלד: עס ברענט די זון אין פּאָװעטינע,
פֿון גרינע היילן שורשען צווישן וואָרצלען גרינע טרערן.

ווען די גרינע אויגנפּאָר וואָלט אונטערגיין אויף אייביק,
אַנשטאַט אַן אייביק וואָלטן זײַן צעווערעמטע סעקונדן.
איך בלאָנדזשע אין אַ וואַלד: ס'איז נאַכט. אַ וואָרצל שלאָגט נאָך גלייביק,
די זון אין פּאָװעטינע איז נאָך אַלץ דאָ ניט פֿאַרשוווּנדן.

זיי זעען מיך, די טונקל גרינע, וואַרטן אויף אַ סימן.
זיי ציטערן ביינאַנד מיט זייער פּנים וויזאַווי מיר.
און שורשענדיקע טרערן פֿון די גרינע היילן שווימען
אַרײַן אין מײַנע זעונגען און לאָזן זייער גלי מיר.

Draw a thread through a needle? No,
even on a stormy night such a struggle isn't worth much:
You have to draw yourself through, you yourself the thread,
and pray that the wonder-needle remains auspicious.

And everything that's not possible will then be possible
and you, the thread, will grasp the prayer of parts.
Wandering, astray, they will come to you. In you. On your
     paths.
You will snuggle with them and heal. Heal. Heal.

With all of your might sew up the wounds, the hanging
ruptures, hanging on gates and chimneys.
Sew up and do justice to the knifed conscience
of your uninvited two-footed dreams.

A language with its song tore its garments, mourning in a
     field,
before wandering lips could drink it up.
Sew up that too! In honor of earlier, childish syllables,
in honor of that first pomegranate and the juice of its
     sparkles.

אריבנציִען אַ פֿאָדעם אין אַ נאָדל? ניין, בן־אָדם.
אַפֿילו אין אַ שטורעמנאַכט אַזאַ פֿאַרמעסט איז ווינציק:
דאַרפֿסט **זיך** אַליין אַריבנציִען, אַליין צו זײַן דער פֿאָדעם
און תּפֿילה טאָן, די ווונדער־נאָדל זאָל דיר בלײַבן גינציק.

און אַלצדינג וואָס ניט מעגלעך וועט שוין יעמאָלט ווערן מעגלעך
און דו, דער פֿאָדעם, וועסט פֿאַרנעמען דאָס געבעט פֿון טײַלן.
דערבלאָנדשען וועלן זיי צו דיר. אין דיר. אויף דײַנע שטעגלעך.
צוזאַמענטוליִען זאָלסטו זיי און הײַלן. הײַלן. הײַלן.

מיט לײַב־און־לעבן דײַנס פֿאַרניי די ווונדן און די ריסן
צעהאַנגענע, געהאַנגענע אויף טויערן און קומענס.
פֿאַרניי און גיב אַ תּיקון דעם צעמעסערטן געוויסן
פֿון דײַנע אומגעבעטענע צוווייפֿיסיקע חלומות.

אַ לשון האָט מיט זײַן געזאַנג אין פֿעלד געריסן קריעה
נאָך איידער ס'האָבן וואָגלענדיקע ליפֿן אים געטרונקען.
פֿאַרניי אים אויך! לכּבֿוד זילבן קינדערישע, פֿריִע,
לכּבֿוד ערשטן מילגרוים און דעם זאַפֿט פֿון זײַנע פֿונקען.

1976

I remember Pasternak: the earth of his forelock
in fresh Moscow snow. A red scarf around his neck,
as if Pushkin had just walked in and taken over.
The snow was still on the ground.

His hand in mine, as if entrusting his key
of fingers to me. His face opposite mine—frightened
and strong. "Go on. I understand the words . . . sounds."
The snow was still on the ground.

I was reading my embers snatched from hell. "*A rege
iz gefaln vi a shtern.*" "A *rege* fell like a star."
He followed me but couldn't grasp *rege*.
The snow was still on the ground.

That *rege* was shining like a star in his pupils
of black marble—moist and polished. In that moment,
the Russian poet was wearing a yellow star.
The snow was still on the ground.

rege—moment

(handwritten annotations: "Russian"; "Artist to Artist"; "to creativity"; "Connection"; "His poems"; "To russians"; "spark"; "Dead"; "Tomb"; "Holocaust"; "Pasternak didn't have to wear them"; "By passing the star, he now get his stories")

דערמאָנונג וועגן פּאַסטערנאַק: די ערד פֿון זײַן טשופֿרינע—
אין פֿרישן מאָסקװער שניי. אַרום דעם האַלדז אַ רױטער שאַליק.
אַזױ װי פּושקין װאָלט אַרײַן . . . עס האָט אים װאָס געפֿאַנגען.
דער שניי איז ניט צעגאַנגען.

זײַן האַנט אין מײַנער, װי ער װאָלט אַ פֿינגערדיקן שליסל
פֿאַרטרױט מיר. און זײַן פּנים, קעגן איבער: אי דערשראָקן
אי מאַכטיק: לייַענט װײַטער, איך פֿאַרשטיי די װערטער, קלאָנגען.
דער שניי איז ניט צעגאַנגען.

איך האָב געלייַענט מײַן גערעטעװעטן זשאַר פֿון גיהנום:
,,אַ רגע איז געפֿאַלן װי אַ שטערן‏''—אַלע װערטער
פֿאַרשטאַנען, חוץ ,,אַ רגע‏''. ניט געקענט צו איר דערלאַנגען.
דער שניי איז ניט צעגאַנגען.

אין זײַנע פֿיכט־געשליפֿענע שװאַרץ־מירמלנע שװאַרצאַפֿלען
האָט אָפּגעשטערנט יענע רגע. און זי האָט אַ רגע
דעם רוסישן פּאָעט מיט געלער לאַטע אױך באַהאַנגען.
דער שניי איז ניט צעגאַנגען.

171

1980

And if I go in winter on a pilgrimage to my hometown,
myself my own double, as now in my thoughts,
I will make my pilgrimage through black snows to that
    cemetery
where the wrinkles of my rescuer Janowa are hovering.

I will read in a whisper, she will hear in a whisper:
Thank you, you have saved my tears from the bonfire.
The tree I have planted for your sake is not enough;
thank you, you have saved both children and grandchildren.

The wheel of time will quickly turn back, even faster,
nightmarish, like my swirling through nooses and through
    claws.
And you, my rescuer, will hide me in a cellar,
You—you, to whom I am making a pilgrimage in my
    thoughts.

A crunch of snow, familiar to me; . . . you in slippers
will go down from the yard to the cellar where I lie, dejected,
again bringing milk, a hunk of bread, and you will cross
    yourself,
and once again I promise I will tell it to my pencil.

און וועל איך צו מײַן היימשטאָט עולה־רגל זײַן אום ווינטער
מיט זיך אַליין אין צוויייען, ווי אַצינד אין דער מחשבֿה,
דורך שוואַרצע שנייען וועל איך עולה־רגל זײַן צום צווינטער
ווו ס׳הויערן די קנייטשן פֿון מײַן רעטערין יאַנאָווע.

בלחש וועל איך לייענען, בלחש וועט זי הערן:
אַ דאַנק, דו האָסט גערעטעוועט פֿון שיטער מײַנע טרערן.
דאָס ביימעלע וואָס כ׳האָב געפֿלאַנצט פֿאַר דיינט וועגן איז ווייניקלעך,
אַ דאַנק, דו האָסט גערעטעוועט סײַ קינדער און סײַ אייניקלעך.

די צעיטראַד וועט געשווינד זיך טאָן אַ דרײ צוריק, נאָך שנעלער,
קאָשמאַרישער, ווי מײַן געדריי דורך פּעטליעס און דורך נעגל.
און דו, מײַן רעטערין, וועסט מיך באַהאַלטן אין אַ קעלער,
דו־דו, וואָס אין געדאַנק בין איך צו דיר שוין עולה־רגל.

אַ סקריפּ אין שנײַ זאָל זײַן מיר קענטלעך, וועסטו אין פּאַנטאָפֿל
אַרײַן פֿון הויף אין קעלער ווו איך ליג פֿאַרזונקען־שפֿל.
און ווידער ברענגען מילך, אַ לוסטע ברויט, און וועסט זיך צלמען,
און ווידער וועל איך צוזאָגן מײַן בליִער צו דערצײַלן אים.

1981

It belongs to me, that hacked-off hand I found
years ago in a garden among tomatoes. Since it
is a man's hand that has no owner, it belongs to me.
A third hand. I can't write a single letter without it.

For my handful of curious readers, I confess:
I am not the one who feeds them magic speech
and who confides reminiscences into a paper ear,
but it is my third hand, found in a garden among tomatoes.

To read what it is writing, it is not enough to know Yiddish.
I myself am learning its language. I wander alone, startled
at night on its paths, fall on stones and thorns,
and in the crack of dawn see it gleaming among tomatoes.

It belongs to me, the hacked-off hand that,
perhaps, caressed a young woman when
its owner was torn apart. And I found it
September, 1941, among tomatoes.

ס׳געהערט צו מיר די אָפּגעהאַקטע האַנט, וואָס קריק מיט יאָרן
געפֿונען האָב איך זי אין גאָרטן צווישן פּאָמידאָרן.
און ווײַל זי איז אַ מענערהאַנט וואָס האָט קיין בעל־הבית ניט
געהערט זי מיר. אַ דריטע האַנט. איך שרײַב אָן איר קיין אות ניט.

פֿאַר נײַגעריקע לייענער אַ צענדליק בין איך מודה:
ניט איך בין זי דער וואָס קאַרמע זיי מיט כּישוף־רייד און סודע
אַרײַן אין אויער פֿון פּאַפּיר ניט־מיינעמס אַ זכרון:
דאָס טוט מײַן דריטע האַנט, געפֿונען צווישן פּאָמידאָרן.

צו לייענען איר שריפֿט איז ניט גענוג צו קענען ייִדיש,
איך לערן זיך אַליין איר לשון. בלאַנדזשע אום יחידיש
בײַ נאַכט אויף אירע שטעגעלעך און פֿאַל אויף שטיין און דאָרן,
באַגיגנען זע איך זי אין זריחה צווישן פּאָמידאָרן.

ס׳געהערט צו מיר די אָפּגעהאַקטע האַנט וואָס האָט געצערטלט,
קאָן זײַן, אַ יונגע פֿרוי, וווען מ׳האָט איר בעל־הבית צעפֿערטלט.
און איך האָב זי געפֿונען ווען דער מאַן האָט זי פֿאַרלאָרן
סעפּטעמבער נײַנצן איין און פֿערציק צווישן פּאָמידאָרן.

"Death redeems death from its captivity, life,
and who redeems life?"—I found these one and a half lines
under ruins in the Vilna earth: on one of the streets
in that city I call my secret city.

There is a gong of silence in a person. And a tremble
reminds itself: It is time to strike it, time to remind the gong.
Now that gong has awakened me. And circles, circles
of captor-doves bring the line and a half to me.

Lend me your thoughts, unknown victim,
to finish what you began and to question:
The word redeems the word from its captivity, the poet,
and who redeems the poet? My question coming off of your
     question.   * resilionce

And again a gong of silence longs for a new trembling,
to remind itself anew and redeem the longing in the line
and a half and confide to their guardian:
The word redeems the word from its captivity . . .

,,דער טויט לייזט אויס דעם טויט פֿון זײַן געפֿענקעניש, דאָס לעבן,
און װער לייזט אויס דאָס לעבן?"—כ'האָב די אָנדערטהאַלבן שורות
געפֿונען אונטער חורבֿות אין דער װילנער ערד: אױף איינער
פֿון אירע גאַסן אין דער שטאָט װאָס הייסט בײַ מיר געהיימשטאָט.

פֿאַראַן אַ גאַנג פֿון שטילקייט אין אַ מענטשן. און אַ ציטער
דערמאָנט זיך: צײַט אים אױפֿצורירן, צײַט אים צו דערמאָנען.
אַצינד האָט אױפֿגעװאַכט אין מיר דער גאַנג. און רינגען, רינגען
אַרײַנפֿאַנג־טויבן ברענגען מיר די אָנדערטהאַלבן שורות.

אָנטלײַ מיר די געדאַנקען דײַנע, אומבאַקאַנטער קרבן,
צו ענדיקן װאָס דו האָסט אָנגעהויבן און צו פֿרעגן:
דאָס װאָרט לייזט אויס דאָס װאָרט פֿון זײַן געפֿענקעניש, דעם דיכטער,
און װער לייזט אויס דעם דיכטער? ס'איז מײַן שאלה אױף דײַן שאלה.

און װידער בענקט אַ גאַנג פֿון שטילקייט נאָך אַ נײַעם ציטער,
דערמאָנען זאָל ער זיך אױף ס'נײַ צו אויסלײַזן די בענקעניש
פֿון אָנדערטהאַלבן שורות און פֿאַרטרויען זײער היטער:
דאָס װאָרט לייזט אויס דאָס װאָרט פֿון זײַן געפֿענקעניש . . .

(For Yosl Berger)

A woman points out to her little boy: "That man over there at
	the table, the one
in the white hat. He's not a man." "So what is he?" "A
	legend."
The little boy turns his head. Mother, child, disappear.
And the sunset sways on her long earrings.

The man at the table, says the woman, is a legend.
A phoenix-man born from the ash heap of a bonfire
is indeed a legend. Only why is that legend
continually thirsty for the young murmuring of sounds?

Why is that legend never-ending and at the same time
in wounds, as if in a hospital while a knife wanders
around in the body and without a compass looks for an
	escape
through a labyrinth of blood vessels, a radiant core?

The brand new night is mild and tender, like a freshly
laid egg. And the foot of the Milky Way ready to strike.
The phoenix-man at the table has an urge to bite
his writing hand. He wants to taste his legend.

אַ פֿרוי ווײַזט אָן איר ייִנגעלע: דער דאָזיקער בײַם טישל,
אין ווײַסן הוט, איז ניט קיין מענטש.—טאָ ווער זשע?—אַ לעגענדע.
דאָס ייִנגעלע דרייט אום דאָס קעפּל. מאַמע, קינד, פֿאַרשווינדן.
און ס׳הוידעט זיך אויף אירע לאָנגע אויירינגען די שקיעה.

דער דאָזיקער בײַם טישל, זאָגט די פֿרוי, איז אַ לעגענדע.
אַ פֿעניקסמעענטש געבוירן פֿונעם אַש פֿון שײַטער־הויפֿן
איז טאַקע אַ לעגענדע. נאָר פֿאַר וואָס איז די לעגענדע
כּסדר דאָרשטיק נאָך דער יונגער מורמלעניש פֿון קלאַנגען?

פֿאַר וואָס איז די לעגענדע איבערצײַטיק און אײַנצײַטיק
אין ווונדן, עלעהיי אין אַ שפּיטאָל בשעת אַ מעסער
שפּאַצירט אַרום אין לײַב און ס׳זוכט אַנטרינונג אָן אַ קאָמפּאַס
דורך לאַבירינט פֿון אָדערן אַ פֿינקלענדיקער עיקר?

די שפּאָגל נײַע נאַכט איז לינד און צערטלעך ווי אַן אָקערשט
געלייגטע איי. דער מילכוועג—מיטן פֿוס אים צו דערלאַנגען.
דער פֿעניקסמעענטש בײַם טישל האָט אַ חשק אײַנצובײַסן.
זײַן שרעבנדיקע האַנט. ער וויל פֿאַרזוכן זײַן לעגענדע.

My unborn heir, it's time for us to get acquainted
(may no one else entertain such an acquaintance)
in around a hundred years or a thousand, it's all the same.
The curtain—drawn open. Play! The stage is lit up:

It's unbelievable! We're so alike:
It's unbelievable! I knew myself personally!
You are me in makeup and now play my role,
my stray wail has become a divine voice.

Till my last breath I wrote this drama
my unborn heir should play in my entirety.
My limbs are sealed under sunset sealing wax,
the stage is lit up, and I see my acts once more.

And my deeds on earth, they live on the stage
in around a hundred years or a thousand, it's all the same.
They live in a shattered city, in a ruin:
It is dark in the hall, the stage is brilliantly lit.

מײַן יורש אומגעבוירענער, שוין צײַט צו שליסן קאַנטשאַפֿט
(מעג עמעצן אין מוח ניט אַרײַן אַזאַ באַקאַנטשאַפֿט)
אין הונדערט יאָר אַרום צי טויזנט, אָן אַ נפֿקא־מינה.
דער פֿאָרהאַנג—אָפֿגעצויגן. שפּיל! באַלויכטן איז די בינע:

ס׳איז ממש ניט צו גלייבן, ווי מיר בײדע זענען ענלעך,
ס׳איז ממש ניט צו גלייבן: איך האָב **זיך** געקענט פֿערזענלעך!
דו ביסט מײַן פֿאַרגרימירטער איך און שפּילסט אַצינד מײַן ראָלע,
געוואָרן איז אַ בת־קול מײַן פֿאַרבלאָנדזשעטע יללה.

ביז לעצטן אָטעם האָב איך דאָך געשריבן דעם ספּעקטאַקל
מײַן יורש אומגעבוירענער זאָל שפּילן מײַן סך־הכּל.
פֿאַרזיגלט זענען אונטער שקיעה־טריוואַקס מײַנע גלידער,
באַלויכטן איז די בינע, מײַנע מעשׂים זע איך ווידער.

און מײַנע מעשׂים אויף דער ערד, זיי לעבן אויף דער בינע
אין הונדערט יאָר אַרום צי טויזנט, אָן אַ נפֿקא־מינה.
זיי לעבן אין אַן אויסגעהאַקטער שטאָט, אין אַ רוינע:
ס׳איז פֿינצטער אינעם זאַל, באַלויכטן זוניק איז די בינע.

Memory of three flamingos by Lake Victoria,
who revealed themselves to me in their splendor and glory,
three strings stretched on a wave, and a bow
moving over them, a bow like a rainbow.

Neither violin or lyre will give birth to such music,
clearly nowhere else a trio of instruments like this.
Its master craftsman longed to try out his creation,
to play upon these living strings with his own hand.

A desert has arisen from skeletal days and nights,
I can't forget the music-stringed three flamingos.
Their colors shimmer in the same unveiled pose,
on their same wave, like rosy-fingered dawn.

And what troubles me now is the anxious question:
Do the three flamingos recall to whom they belong?

                    *

Once in a lifetime does fate grant us such an encounter . . .
fated to see such a thing, to hear such a thing.

דערמאָנונג וועגן דרײַ פֿלאַמינגאַס בײַ דער לײַק וויקטאָריע,
וואָס האָבן זיך אַנטהילט פֿאַר מיר אין זייער פּראַכט און גלאָריע:
דרײַ סטרונעס אָנגעשפּאַנטע אויף אַ כוואַליע, און אַ בויגן
באַוועגט זיך איבער זיי, אַ רעגן־בויגנדיקער בויגן.

אַזאַ מוזיק וועט ניט געבוירן פֿידל אָדער לירע,
אַזאַ מין דרײליינג־אינסטרומענט איז ניט בנימצא קעננטיק.
פֿאַרבענקט האָט זיך זיין מײַסטער אויסצופֿרווען זיין יצירה,
צו שפּילן אויף די לעבעדיקע סטרונעס אייגען־העננטיק.

אַ מידבר איז געוואָרן פֿון סקעלעטישע מעת־לעתן,
די סטרונענדיקע דרײַ פֿלאַמינגאַס קאָן איך ניט פֿאַרגעסן.
זיי מיניען זיך אין זעלביקער אַנטפּלעקערישער פּאָזע,
אויף זייער זעלבער כוואַליע, ווי באַגיניען־זון אַ ראָזע.

און וואָס אַצינד מיך טאַטשעט, איז די נײַגעריקע פֿרעגעניש:
דערמאָנען זיך די דרײַ פֿלאַמינגאַס וועמען זיי געהערן?

*

אַן איינציק מאָל אין לעבן איז באַשערט אַזאַ באַגעגעניש,
באַשערט אַזוינס צו זען, אַזוינס צו הערן.

187

1982

Good morning, young drop of blood, good morning to you,
    blood-morning,
a white virginal day is still in my journal
that must be ploughed with joy until night and the warmth
    of sun
so seed it an endless life arises.

Light up my vision, young wandering drop,
vision is my blindness. And light up separately
each delight a generous hand has presented to me:
Once again I want to outlive it on the eve of our parting.

Don't compare it to anything else. Years ago now
I compared it to a tree flayed by a storm.
It's like a goldsmith now, rapt in concentration,
and sparks spurt from the tender hammer of his workshop.

I will fight a duel on account of my jealousy of life,
even testing my luck with Goliath-death.
Both will hide in the white day of my journal.
Good morning wandering drop of blood, good morning,
    blood-morning.

גוט־מאָרגן יונגער טראָפּן בלוט, גוט־מאָרגן דיר, בלוט־מאָרגן,
אַ וויסער בתולהדיקער טאָג איז נאָך פֿאַראַן אין טאָגבוך
וואָס דאַרף מיט פֿרייד געאַקערט ווערן ביז דער נאַכט און זוניק
פֿאַרזייט ווערן, אַז אויפֿגיין זאָל אַ לעבן וואָס איז אייביק.

באַליכט מײַן זעעוודיקייט, יונגער, בלאַנדזשענדיקער טראָפּן,
די זעעוודיקייט איז מײַן בלינדקייט. און באַליכט באַזונדער
מײַן יעדן תּענוג וואָס אַ האַנט אַ ברייטע האָט געשאַנקען:
כ׳וויל נאָך אַ מאָל אים איבערלעבן ערבֿ אונדזער אָפּשייד.

פֿאַרגליכן אים ניט מיט קיינעמען. איך האָב אים שוין פֿאַרגליכן
צוריק מיט יאָרן צו אַ בוים געשונדן פֿון אַ שטורעם.
אַ גאָלדשמיד איז ער איצטער, אַ פֿאַרזונקענער אין מוח,
און פֿונקען שפּריצן פֿון זײַן צאַרטן העמערל בײַם וואַרשטאַט.

כ׳וועל גיין אויף אַ דועל צוליב דער אײַפֿערזוכט צום לעבן
אַפֿילו מיטן גליתדיקן טויט און פֿרוּוון מזל.
אין וויסן טאָג פֿון טאָגבוך וועלן ביידע זיך פֿאַרבאָרגן.
דו בלאַנדזשענדיקער טראָפּן בלוט, גוט־מאָרגן דיר, גוט־מאָרגן.

When your words, rhymes, will quiver into their death
        throes,
and your lips will look like beggars in a desert,
even your thoughts unable to follow your ruminations,
and you will long for a snakebite as if it's liberation,

then for the first time that new language will hatch in you
and enable you to carry on a conversation with an olive tree,
enable you to fall in love with the dancer of a storm,
and to blow a springtime into a valley of dead words.

Then for the first time will you be able to write to King
        Solomon
and wait for an ant to bring back his wisdom, signed and sealed,
and what will outweigh everything else in the scales is a
        certainty:
there is no more beautiful life than this life.

Then for the first time will you become acquainted with a
        mirror
with cats-eyes when a Hiroshima leaps out from them.
And you will wander in coral-cities and speak to corals
where a star-angel has still not yet fallen.

ווען אויסגעגוססט וועלן צאַנקען דײַנע ווערטער, גראַמען,
און בעטלערס אין אַ מידבר וועלן אויסזען דײַנע ליפן,
אַפֿילו דײַן געדאַנק וועט ניט פֿאַרשטיין וואָס דו וועסט קלערן
און בענקען וועסטו נאָך אַ שלאָנגענביס ווי נאָך באַפֿרײַונג,

ערשט יעמאָלט וועט זיך אויספיקן אין דיר דאָס נײַע לשון
צו קענען מיט אַן אײַלבערטבוים פֿאַרלענגערן אַ שמועס,
צו קענען זיך פֿאַרליבן אין דער טענצערין פֿון שטורעם,
אַרײַנבלאָזן אַ פֿרילינג אין אַ טאָל פֿון טויטע ווערטער.

ערשט יעמאָלט וועסטו קענען שרײַבן צו דעם קיניג שלמה
און וואַרטן, אַ מוראשקע זאָל צוריקברענגען פֿאַרזיגלט
זײַן חכמה, אַז אַריבערוועגן זאָל בײַ דיר אין וואָגשאָל
אַ זיכערקייט: ניטאָ קיין שענער לעבן ווי דאָס לעבן.

ערשט יעמאָלט וועסטו קענען שליסן קאָנטשאַפֿט מיט אַ שפּיגל,
מיט קאַצנאויגן ווען אין זיי צעשפּרינגט אַ הירשאָמ.
און וואָגלען אין קאָראָלן־שטעטעל און ריידן צו קאָראַלן
וווהין אַ שטערן־מלאך איז נאָך קיין מאָל ניט געפֿאַלן.

"How come you don't mention your Siberian father in your
    diary poems?"
A question just came to me. Instead of an answer, Look:
Before my very eyes his skin has covered my own,
and before my very eyes his beard has grown on me.

And now that aloof son—has become his own father.
With his fingers I roll loose tobacco in a paper casing.
The night is on a sparkling grindstone, ruddy and clear.
How come I know by heart page after page of the Talmud?

How come I can play the violin? I play with his fingers;
the unearthly strings have memories of the Garden of Eden.
Whose spade is that, glazed with sparkling ice?
With his bony fingers I play on his violin.

We've become eternal in the same small space,
the old snow falling youthfully and blanketing us both,
rifles and cannons no longer able to separate us.

"How come you don't mention your Siberian father in your
    diary poems?"

,,אַלמאַי דערמאָנסטו ניט אין טאָגבוך דײַן סיבירער טאַטן?''
געקומען איז אַ שאלה. און אַנשטאָט אן ענטפער, זע נאָר:
פֿאַר מײַנע אויגן האָט זײַן הויט אויף מײַנער זיך באַצויגן
און אויסגעוואָקסן איז אויף מיר זײַן באַרד פֿאַר מײַנע אויגן.

אַצינד איז גאָר זײַן זון דער אָפּגעזונדערטער—זײַן טאַטע,
איך דרײַ מיט זײַנע פֿינגער ווי כן טאַביק אין אַ גילזע,
די נאַכט איז אויף אַ שליפֿראָד אַ צעפֿונקטע, ראָזלעך קלאָרע.
פֿון וואַנען קען איך אויסנווייניק בלאָט נאָך בלאַט גמרא?

פֿון וואַנען קען איך שפּילן פֿידל? כ׳שפּיל מיט זײַנע פֿינגער,
יענוועלטיקע די סטרונעס מיט זכרון פֿון גן־עדן.
פֿאַרשאַטן מיט אַ פֿינקלענדיקן אויג, האָט וועמעס רידל?
מיט זײַנע ביינערדיקע פֿינגער שפּיל איך אויף זײַן פֿידל.

מיר זענען צוגעאײיביקט צו די זעלבע דלת אמות,
דער אַלטער שניי האָט יונגן כוח בײַדן צו פֿאַרשנייען,
צעשיידן קאָנען אונדז ניט מער קיין ביקסן און האַרמאַטן.

*

,,אַלמאַי דערמאָנסטו ניט אין טאָגבוך דײַן סיבירער טאַטן?''

1983

A distant morning's anthem by a poet yet to be born.
Consecrated, one and only, in my blazing imagination,
you won't employ habitual old words.
Let the storm be a classic author for you. Like him,

write with lightning on parchment clouds. Make a vow:
you won't stop writing on those clouds until
my white dust comes alive and I can float to them.
Give me a sign: There is no death. We both are alive.

Consecrated in my blazing imagination, skeletons by the
    millions
stiffening in the earth—you are their milk and honey.
Take pity on humankind under tree and tower.
Give me a sign: For you the storm is a classic author.

Enough—diluting the lamentation with tired tears,
Enough—threading pearls for a throat no longer here,
Enough—overturning tiny worlds with feathered quills from
    the golden peacock.
A human being wants to gulp your lightning like a watermelon.

דעם ניט־געבוירערענעם פּאָעט אין מאָרגנווײַט אַ הימען.

געזאַלבטער, אײַ־און־אײַנציקער אין מײַן צעגגליטן דמיון,
קיין צוגעוווינטע אַלטע ווערטער זאָלסטו ניט באַניצן,
אַ קלאַסיקער זאָל זײַן פֿאַר דיר דער שטורעם. שרײַב מיט בליצן

אַזוי ווי ער אויף אויף פֿאַרמעטענע וואָלקנס! טו אַ נדר:
דו וועסט ניט אויפֿהערן צו שרײַבן אויף די וואָלקנס אײַדער
מײַן וויסער שטויב איז לעבעדיק, איך זאָל צו זיי דערשוועבן.
באַוויַיז אַ צייכן: ס'איז ניטאָ קיין טויט. מיר ביידע לעבן.

געזאַלבטער אין צעגגליטן דמיון, ס'גליווערן מיליאָניק
סקעלעטן אין דער ערד און דו—ביסט זייער מילך און האָניק.
דערבאַרעם זיך אויף מענטשנקינדער אונטער בוים און טורעם,
באַוויַיז אַ צייכן: ס'איז פֿאַר דיר אַ קלאַסיקער דער שטורעם.

גענוג מיט מידע טרערן צו פֿאַרוואַסערן דעם יאָמער,
גענוג צו סיליען פֿערל פֿאַר אַ האָלדז וואָס איז ניטאָ מער,
גענוג צו קערן וועלטעלעך מיט פֿעדערן גאָלד־פֿאַוועני:
אַ מענטשנקינד וויל שלינגען דײַנע בליצן ווי אַ קאַווענע.

Not even the least of things was crushed under your shoes,
whatever lost is found by you outside or in you.
Where the roots of the tree in the Garden of Eden draw
        inspiration,
lips, without words, draw nearer to the tree of joy.

Blue eyes of a snowman . . . and they glow so much
you feel the North Star will also soon come in its equipage.
A little dove brings a greeting from before-you-were born,
and long rolled-away days and nights hurry back to your
        domain.

Shaped by earth, without words say thank you to the earth,
she brought forth her berries also for your thought.
And your very first dream visits you in a dream,
and your very last dream is pledged to the first one.

ניט צעטראָטן איז דאָס מינדסטע אונטער דײַנע שיך,
וואָס פֿאַרלוירן דאָס געפֿינסטו צי אין דרויסן צי אין זיך.
וווּ עס ציען די יניקה וואָרצלען פֿון גן־עדן־בוים
ציען ליפֿן זיך בשתיקה נעענטער צום פֿרײַדנבוים.

בלויע אויגן פֿון אַ שנײַמעענטש . . . און זײַ גליען אַזש,
באַלד וועט אויך דער צפֿון־שטערן קומען אין זײַן עקיפּאַזש.
פֿונעם איידער־דײַן־געבוירן ברענגט אַ טײַבעלע אַ גרוס,
לאַנג פֿאַרקײַקלטע מעת־לעתן אײַלן זיך צו דײַן רשות.

ערד באַשאַפֿענער, אָן ווערטער זאָג דער ערד אַ דאַנק,
אויסגעוואָרעמט אירע יאָגדעס האָט זי אויך פֿאַר דײַן געדאַנק.
און דער ערשטער חלום דײַנער קומט אין חלום דיר צו גאַסט,
און דער לעצטער חלום דײַנער מיטן ערשטן איז פֿאַרקנסט.

Ever since my pious mother ate earth on Yom Kippur,
black earth mixed with fire on Yom Kippur,
I, among the living, must eat black earth on Yom Kippur,
I myself a memorial candle kindled by her fire.

The masts sink without any pity from the setting sun.
Like a bird, a star scurries to a second star.
But ever since my mother ate earth on Yom Kippur instead of
        fasting,
I too must eat earth Yom Kippur after Yom Kippur.

A locust left no more on my lips than
the stalks of two syllables from a single word: mama.
On their own, my lips swim to my pious mother,
where she fasted on another shore.

The silence between us grows more silent. Silent to its depths.
And she who eats earth on Yom Kippur grasps her son's
        thoughts
and prays that her prayer will shield her son
when the memorial candle starts to flicker.

פֿון זינט מײַן פֿרומע מאַמע האָט געגעסן ערד יום־כּיפּור,
געגעסן אום יום־כּיפּור שוואַרצע ערד געמישט מיט פֿײַער,
אַ לעבעדיקער, מוז איך עסן שוואַרצע ערד יום־כּיפּור,
און בין אַליין אַ יאָרצײַט־ליכט געצונדן פֿון איר פֿײַער.

ס׳פֿאַרזינקען אומדערבאַרעמדיק פֿון זונפֿאַרגאַנג די מאַסטן,
אַ שטערן צו אַ צווייטן שטערן פֿױגליש טוט אַ היפּער,
נאָר זינט מײַן מאַמע עסט יום־כּיפּור ערד אַנשטאָט צו פֿאַסטן,
פֿון יעמאָלט מוז איך עסן ערד יום־כּיפּור נאָך יום־כּיפּור.

אַ הײשעריק האָט ניט געלאָזן מער אױף מײַנע ליפּן,
װי זאַנגענע צװײ זילבן פֿון אַ װאָרט אַן איינציקס: מאַמע.
באַזונדער פֿון מײַן ליב־און־לעבן שװימען זיי, די ליפּן,
צום קינױגריכיך װי ס׳האָט געפֿאַסט אַ מאָל מײַן פֿרומע מאַמע.

די שטילקייט צווישן אונדז װערט שטילער. ביז צום דנאָ אַ שטילע.
און די װאָס עסט יום־כּיפּור ערד פֿאַרנעמט איר זונס געדאַנקען
און תּפֿילה טוט זי, אַז אים זאָל באַשירעמען איר תּפֿילה
בשעת די יאָרצײַט־ליכט וועט נעמען צאַנקען.

*(For my friend Rokhl Krinski-Melezin, who reminded me
that I asked a surgeon in the Vilna Ghetto Hospital to let
me be present at a brain operation.)*

Tell me, what did you want to see in that skull
cut open when the Jewish city had already been cut to pieces?
"Probably to see the eternal that remains outside of death;
I even have a name for it: radiant core."

That skull—open. Its armor wasn't so thick.
Now—my fate—to see its radiant core.
The world must have appeared like that at its Creation,
light bearing light. Bore and was born.

That skull—open. And I look into its abyss
after the old Jewish city had been cut to pieces:
thin veins of script. I see the name-without-a-name.
I shade my eyes. I see that radiant core.

The hospital's turned dark. It's sinking to its knees.
The skull of the city is open. I've nowhere to run off to.
I'm drunk from my vision, dead drunk.
Now this radiant core will protect me

פֿאַר מײַן פֿרײַנד רחל קרינסקי־מעלעזין, וואָס האָט מיר דערמאָנט,
אַז כ׳האָב געגעבטן אַ כירורג אַ כירורג ער זאָל מיר דערלויבן בײַצוזײַן אין
ווילנער געטאָ־שפּיטאָל בײַ אַ מוח־אָפּעראַצִיע.

דערצײַל, וואָס האָסטו זען געוואַלט בײַם אויפֿשנײַדן אַ שאַרבן
ווען שוין צעשניטן איז געווען די ייִדנשטאָט אויף שטיקער?
—מסתמא זען דאָס אײַביקע וואָס בלײַבט מחוצן שטאַרבן,
אַ נאָמען האָב איך עס געגעבן: פֿינקלענדיקער עיקר.

דער שאַרבן—אָפֿן. ס׳איז דער פֿאַנצער זײַנער ניט קיין דיקער,
אַצינד באַשערט איז מיר צו זען זײַן פֿינקלענדיקן עיקר.
אַזוי האָט קענטיק אויסגעזען די וועלט בײַם בראשית־ברא,
אַזוי האָט ליכט געבוירן ליכט. געבוירן און געבאָרן.

דער שאַרבן—אָפֿן. און איך קוק אַרײַן אין זײַנע תּהומען
ווען שוין צעשניטן איז די אַלטע ייִדנשטאָט אויף שטיקער:
דײַן־אָדערדיקע שריפֿט. איך זע דעם נאָמען־אָן־אַ־נאָמען,
פֿאַרשטעל איך מײַנע אויגן: ס׳איז דער פֿינקלענדיקער עיקר.

פֿאַרלאָשן דער שפּיטאָל. עס נעמען קנײַען זײַנע זײַלן.
דער שאַרבן פֿון דער שטאָט איז אָפֿן. כ׳האָב ניט וווּ צו אײַלן.
און שיכּור בין איך פֿון דער זעונג, ביז משוגע שיכּור:
אַצינד וועט מיך באַשירעמען דער פֿינקלענדיקער עיקר.

I am your abyss, your ash and hell . . .
I am your very last look. Recognize it.

I am your last spark. I say goodbye
and want to ignite a rainfall with it.

I am the heir of your first love,
the green jealousy of those whom you love.

I am a diary. You dance on its leaves.
A demon claps out from the storm: Divine!

Your breath is my bread and I—a knife.
This kind of bread belongs only to me—its eater.

I am a purple hospital in sunset
in which your eyelash still quivers.

I am a woodpecker in a forest of stars.
I peck out from myself the tears.

I am your young death. And wherever I find myself:
Your skeleton is inside of me. I wear it in my self.

איך בין דײַן אָפּגרונט, בין דײַן אַש און גיהנום,
איך בין דײַן סאַמע לעצטער בליק, דערקען אים.

איך בין דײַן לעצטער פֿונק, וואָס איך געזאָגן
און אָנצינדן איך וויל מיט אים אַ רעגן.

איך בין דער יורש פֿון דײַן ערשטער ליבע,
די גרינע אײַפֿערזוכט פֿון דײַנע ליבע.

איך בין אַ טאָגבוך. טאָנצסט אויף זײַנע בלעטלעך,
אַ דעמאָן פּאַטשט אַרויס פֿון שטורעם: געטלעך!

דײַן אָטעם איז מײַן ברויט און איך—אַ מעסער,
אַזאַ מין ברויט געהערט בלויז מיר, זײַן עסער.

איך בין אַ פֿורפֿלנער שפּיטאָל אין שקיעה
וווּ אינעוווייניק ציטערט נאָך דײַן וויע.

איך בין אַ פֿיקהאָלץ אין אַ וואַלד פֿון שטערן,
איך פֿיק אַרויס פֿון זיך אַליין די טרערן.

איך בין דײַן יונגער טויט. און וווּ כ׳געפֿין זיך:
אין מיר איז דײַן סקעלעט. איך טראָג אים אים אינזיך.

I read texts that a man's hand is incapable of writing.
Hastily, they flash by. I look for a name.
They are barely like seagulls on the eve of a deluge,
the ocean about to heave up treasures from its abyss.

I was born to know how to read them, those texts,
and I must constantly lie in wait for their favor and goodwill.
Dispatched from some remoter place, far away,
they cleave the night-granite, revelatory and dazzling.

Delaying for an instant will deprive me of my good fortune
to read the letters that no one else has seen.
And at the end of such days my eyelash won't be able
to stay open, and my bones will lie dead.

In rare seconds I can capture them, and thread the texts
onto paper, only, to tell the truth, I don't know
whom they belong to. And I ask them to forgive me
while I write above them, "Avrom," though I don't know
        whose . . .

איך לייען טעקסטן וואָס אַ מענטשנהאַנט איז ניט קאַפּאַבל
צו שרײבן. האַסטיק בליצן זיי פֿאַרבײַ. איך זוך אַ נאָמען.
זיי זענען ענלעכע קוים־קוים צו מעוואָס ערבֿ מבול
בשעת דער ים וועט באַלד אַ הייב טאָן אוצרות פֿון די תהומען.

געבוירן בין איך זיי צו קענען לייענען, די טעקסטן,
כ'מוז לאָקערן אויף זייער גנאָד און גינציקייט באַשטענדיק.
אַרויסגעשיקטע פֿון אַ ווײַטן העק, דעם סאַמע העקסטן,
צעזעגן זיי דעם נאַכטגראַניט אַנטפֿלעקעריש און בלענדיק.

פֿאַרזאַם איך זיך אַן אויגנבליק, וועט אָפּטאָן זיך מײַן זכיה
צו לייענען די אותיות וואָס דערזען האָט זיי ניט קיינער.
און ס'וועט בײַם אויסלאָז פֿון די טעג ניט קאָנען זיך מײַן וויע
אַן עפֿן טאָן, און בלײַבן טויטע וועלן מײַנע בײַנער.

אין זעלטענע סעקונדעס קאָן איך פֿאַנגען זיי, און צילע
אַרויף די טעקסטן אויף פּאַפּיר, נאָר כ'ווייס ניט אויף אַן אמת
צו וועמען זיי געהערן. און איך בעט בײַ זיי מחילה,
וואָס אויבן שרײַב איך אָן אבֿרהם, כאַטש איך ווייס ניט וועמעס ...

1984

I still owe you an answer to your letter,
written before you were born. Before you had put on the
    clothing
of spring, summer, fall and winter. Our seasons.
Your dress—of wild red poppy—loves that I remember it.

I still owe you an answer to the coil of your hair: a sign
set afloat by the river, to swim all that distance to me.
A dark gravedigger covers the sunset. A mere breeze
carries to me the odor and the tenderness of your packed
    hair.

And I am guilty because I have also forgotten your address,
even that you are beyond envelopes and addresses.
Even though no one has revealed your second home,
I must answer you with a letter, at least once and for all.

I will cut open a vein and write without words
so you can read, and we will be embodied once again.
A nocturnal river will whirl us together:
The Almighty will be jealous of our pleasures.

איך קום דיר נאָך אַן ענטפֿער אויף דײַן בריוו, געשריבן איידער
דו ביסט געבוירן. איידער דו האָסט אָנגעטאָן די קליידער
פֿון פֿרילינג, זומער, האַרבסט און ווינטער. אונדזערע סעזאָנען.
דײַן קלייד פֿון ווילדן רויטן מאָן האָט ליב איך זאָל דערמאָנען.

איך קום דיר נאָך אַן ענטפֿער אויף דײַן בינטל האָר: אַ סימן
געלאָזן מיטן טײַך, צו מיר דעם וויטן צו דערשווימען.
דעם זונפֿאַרגאַנג פֿאַרשיט אַ שוואַרצער קברן. בלויז אַ ווינטל
דערטראָגט צו מיר דעם ריח און די צאַרטקייט פֿונעם בינטל.

און שולדיק בין איך, וואָס דײַן אַדרעס האָב איך אויף פֿאַרגעסן,
אַפֿילו אַז דו ביסט מחוץ קאָנווערטן און אַדרעסן.
אַפֿילו אַז דײַן צווייטע האַנט איז קיינער ניט מגלה,
איך מוז דיר ענטפֿערן אַ בריוו, כאַטש איינעם אויף די אַלע.

איך וועל זיך אויפֿשנײַדן אַן אָדער און אָן ווערטער שרײַבן
זאָלסט קענען לייענען, און מיר׳ן ווידער זיך פֿאַרלײַבן.
און אַז צוזאַמענקוואַליען וועט אונדז ביידן אַ ביטנאַכטיקער
דער טײַך: מקנא זײַן וועט אונדזער תּענוג דער אַלמאַכטיקער.

The murmur-hieroglyphics on your face are true
legends of my generation.

I read them with eye and ear. Their contents
outweigh libraries.

I read your murmur-hieroglyphics and marvel
at the heroes and victims.

Marvel at a played-out fire,
its last sparks.

I read your murmur-hieroglyphics and bizarrely
recognize the truth of my own life.

Recognize the nail in my soul
and whose hand and hammer drove it in.

Recognize the ladder that elevated me
to the undercurrent in an upside-down abyss.

I live in your murmur-hieroglyphics
as in the first half of my memory.

Recognize in them my unfulfilled delight,
that I inherited in a world without heirs.

I live in your murmur-hieroglyphics
even now, when I read them with eye and ear.

די מורמל־הירעאָגליפֿן אויף דײַן פּנים זענען וואָרע
לעגענדעס פֿון מײַן דור.

איך לייען זיי מיט אויג און אויער. זייער אינהאַלט וועגט
אַריבער ביבליאָטעקן.

איך לייען דײַנע מורמל־הירעאָגליפֿן און באַוווּנדער
די העלדן און קרבנות.

באַוווּנדער אַ פֿאַרשפּילטע שׂרפֿה,
אירע לעצטע פֿונקען.

איך לייען דײַנע מורמל־הירעאָגליפֿן און דערקען
משונה־אמתדיק מײַן אייגן לעבן.

דערקען דעם טשוואָק אין דער נשמה מײַנער
און וועמעס האַנט און האַמער האָבן אים אַרײַנגעשלאָגן.

דערקען דעם ליבטער וואָס האָט מיך דערהויבן
בײַן אונטערשטראָם אין אַ קאַפּויערדיקן אָפּגרונט.

אין דײַנע מורמל־הירעאָגליפֿן לעב איך,
ווי אין דער ערשטער העלפֿט פֿון מײַן זכרון.

דערקען אין זיי מײַן אומגעשטילטן תּענוג,
וואָס כ׳האָב געירשנט אין אַ וועלט אָן יורשים.

אין דײַנע מורמל־הירעאָגליפֿן לעב איך
אַפֿילו איצטער, ווען איך לייען זיי מיט אויג און אויער.

Where are they, the summer darlings: boys, girls,
with sweet sin that has no fear of any Garden of Eden?
The riddle is sealed, the secret is inexplicable,
only I, the magician, will solve the riddle.

They live a separate kind of existence in my words,
not even the least experience lost in these words.
A long time has no authority or influence over them.
Only in them and nowhere else my cherry tree blooms.

Minutes are sifted from the black flour of midnight
when my words open themselves. Only then, without words,
they walk out Lilliputian moon-strollers,
and I recognize the boys, the girls, from the green places.

Then they give signs: "Our joys will not end,
hot blooded we live a constant word-life.
We live a separate kind of life in your words,
not even the least experience lost in these words."

216

ווּ זענען זיי די ליבלינגען פֿון זומער: ייִנגלעך, מיידלעך,
מיט זיסער זינד וואָס האָט ניט מורא פֿאַר קיין שום גן־עדן?
פֿאַרזיגלט איז דאָס רעטעניש, דער סוד איז אומבאַשייידלעך,
נאָר איך, דער כישוף־מאַכער, וועל דאָס רעטעניש באַשיידן:

זיי לעבן אין די ווערטער מיינע אַ באַזונדער לעבעניש,
פֿאַרלוירן ווערט ניט זיי אין די ווערטער ס׳מינדסטע איבערלעבעניש.
אַ שאָק מיט יאָרן האָט אויף זיי קיין דעה און קיין שליטה ניט,
ס׳טוט אַנדערש ווו אַחוץ אין זיי מיַן קאָרשנבוים קיין צוויטע ניט.

פֿון שוואַרצן מעל פֿון האַלבנאַכט ווערן אויסגעזיפט מינוטן
ווען מיַנע ווערטער עפֿענען זיך. יעמאָלט בלויז, אָן ווערטער,
שפּאַצירן זיי אַרויס: לבֿנה־גייערערס־ליליפוטן,
און איך דערקען די ייִנגלעך, מיידלעך, פֿון די גרינע ערטער.

דאָס גיבן זיי סימנים: ס׳וועט זיך אונדזער פֿרייד ניט ענדיקן,
הייסבלוטיק לעבן מיר אַ ווערטער־לעבן אַ באַשטענדיקן.
מיר לעבן אין די ווערטער דיַנע אַ באַזונדער לעבעניש,
פֿאַרלוירן ווערט ניט אין די ווערטער ס׳מינדסטע איבערלעבעניש.

Not one, not two, not how-many-thousands . . . Oh my, so
    many "Nots,"
we stood at night by the red-hot crater.
A mistake, not "We," a half spark in its final quiver
returned, mute-returned, to its home, to the crater.

That half spark was me, and within—all:
not one, not two, not how-many-thousands. Child, and bride
    and groom.
And their souls didn't believe in my Kaddish:
Has a brother really wandered his way back?

Has anyone in the fabric-air torn his clothes in mourning?
No Jews around. Only the waves of the Viliya move.
And I, the half spark by the crater, listen: They go, go,
the waves go, and the Jews stand rigid in rows.

Lava gushes out from the crater over the entire region,
I recognize so many faces I once met sometime ago.
Not one, not two, not how-many-thousands. Oh my, so
    many "Nots"
and I, that half spark, am among them, in the midst of them.

ניט איינס, ניט צוויי, ניט וויפֿל טויזנט. ווייַ, אַזוי פֿיל ניטן
געשטאַנען זענען מיר בײַ נאַכט בײַם קראַעטער דעם צעגליטן.
אַ טעות, ניט קיין 'מיר', אַ האַלבער פֿונק אין לעצטן פֿלאַטער
האָט אומגעקערט זיך, שטומגעקערט זיך צו זײַן היים, צום קראַעטער.

דער האַלבער פֿונק בין **איך** געווען, און אינעוויייניק—אלע:
ניט איינס, ניט צוויי, ניט וויפֿל טויזנט. קינד און חתן־כלה.
און ס'האָבן זייערע נשמות ניט געגלייבט מײַן קדיש:
צי האָט זיך טאַקע אומגעקערט אַ ברודער נע־וָונדיש?

האָט עמעץ אין דער ליטוונטענער לוֹפֿט געריסן קריעה?
ניטאָ קיין ייַדן. ס'גייען בלויז די כוואַליעס אין ווילִיע.
און איך, דער האַלבער פֿונק בײַם קראַעטער, האָרך: זיי גייען, גייען,
די כוואַליעס גייען, און די ייַדן גליוווערן אין רייַען.

פֿון קראַעטער שלאָגט אַרויס אַ לאַווע איבער גאָרער געגנט,
כ'דערקען אַזוי פֿיל פנימער אַ מאָל, אַ מאָל באַאגעגנט:
ניט איינס, ניט צוויי, ניט וויפֿל טויזנט. ווייַ, אַזוי פֿיל ניטן
און איך, דער האַלבער פֿונק, בין צווישן אַלעמען, אין מיטן.

1985

FROM *In Somewhere-Night of Black Honey*

I

Back and forth, they run around, the nurses:
ants in white, only in white.

Armed with safety pins, they carry the secrets
of underground homes, like pits in a dream.

At dawn they bring the sunrise through the corridors:
they saved it from a fire outside.

Ample bosomed, they grant to the innocent prisoners
their curative smiles.

And perhaps they sleep at night with hotheaded angels?
The nurses in white, only in white.

אין ערגעצדיקער נאַכט פֿון שוואַרצן האָניק

א

אַהין און קריק זיי לויפֿן דאָ אַרום די קראַנקן־שוועסטער:
מוראַשקעלעך אין ווײַסן, בלויז אין ווײַסן.

פֿאַרשפּיליעטע מיט זיכער־נאָדלען טראָגן זיי די סודות
פֿון הײמען אונטערערדישע, ווי גריבער אין אַ חלום.

באַגינען ברענגען זיי דורך קאָרידאָרן דעם באַגינען,
זיי האָבן אים געראַטעוועט אין דרויסן פֿון אַ שׂרפֿה.

צו אומשולדיקע אַרעסטאַנטן שענקען זיי בריטעברוסטיק
רפֿואהדיקע שמייכלען.

און אפֿשר שלאָפֿן זיי בײַ נאַכט מיט היציקע מלאָכים?
די שוועסטערלעך אין ווײַסן, בלויז אין ווײַסן.

223

2

With golden needles the sun knits
a cloud.
Raindrops fall to brighten
an old bent headstone,
a wrinkled headstone,
somewhere in a remote moldering cemetery
where its Hebrew hieroglyphics rinse away
in carbonized time
and let hunchbacked tears hang.
Now an heir will be able to read the name
of the sacred skeleton.
But no one is there in that moldering cemetery
except the corpses. But the corpses are also not there.
And among those not there is also
the heir.

מיט שפּיזלען גילדענע שטריקט אויס די זון
אַ וואָלקן.
ס׳פֿאַלן רעגן־טראָפּנס צו דערפֿרייען
אַן אַלטע אײַנגעבויגענע מצבֿה
אַ צעקנייטשטע
ערגעץ אויף אַ וויסטלעכן פֿאַרשימלטן בית־עלמין,
שוועֶנקען אָפּ פֿון אירע היעראָגליפֿן די העברעישע
פֿאַרקוילטע צײַט, און לאָזן העֶנגֶען הויקעֶרדיקע טרערן.
איצטער וועט אַ יורש קעֶנען לייענען דעם נאָמען
פֿון הייליקן סקעֶלעט.
נאָר קיינער איז ניטאָ אויף דעם פֿאַרלעֶגענעם בית־עלמין
אַחוץ די מתים. נאָר די מתים זעֶנען אויך ניטאָ.
און צווישן די ניטאָיקע איז אויך ניטאָ
דער יורש.

6

When my memory will move out from me,
like somebody moving from one apartment
to another,
what will happen?
My memory will become a cloud, a cloud
ploughed by lightning
and seeded with droplets of rain.
And a rainfall of blessing
will grow from it,
will grow and fall on you, in you.

My memory will become a rainfall of blessing.

ווען אַרויסקליַיבן וועט זיך פֿון מיר מיַין זכרון,
װי אַ מענטש פֿון זיַין דירה
אין אַ צוויַיטער, אַן אַנדערער,
װאָס וועט געשען?
מיַין זכרון וועט ווערן אַ װאָלקן, אַ װאָלקן
מיט בליצן געאַקערט און טראָפּעלעך רעגן
פֿאַרזייט.
און אויפֿגייין פֿון אים וועט אַ רעגן פֿון ברכה,
אויפֿגייין און פֿאַלן אויף דיר, אין דיר.

מיַין זכרון וועט ווערן אַ רעגן פֿון ברכה.

It was worthwhile, and will still be worthwhile,
to reside in a drop of dew,
reside in it to the last breath.

A gathering of one, of two, of life itself,
as long as you reside there and see
how suns alternate their crowns.

It was worthwhile, and will still be worthwhile,
to reside in a drop of dew
far from the somebodies,

when stars wrestle with wolves
over fields and plains.
It was worthwhile, and will still be worthwhile.

ס'האָט געלוינט, ס'וועט נאָך לוינען,

צו ווינען אין אַ טראָפן טוי, ביז לעצטן אָטעם ווינען.

זאַלבע אײן, זאַלבע צווײ, זאַלבע לעבן, אַבי דאָרטן ווינען

און זען ווי עס בּיטן זיך זונען מיט זײערע קרוינען.

ס'האָט געלוינט, ס'וועט נאָך לוינען,

צו ווינען אין אַ טראָפן טוי באַזונדער פֿון פֿאַרשוינען,

ווען עס ראַנגלען זיך שטערן מיט וועלף איבער וועלדער און פֿלוינען.

ס'האָט געלוינט, ס'וועט נאָך לוינען.

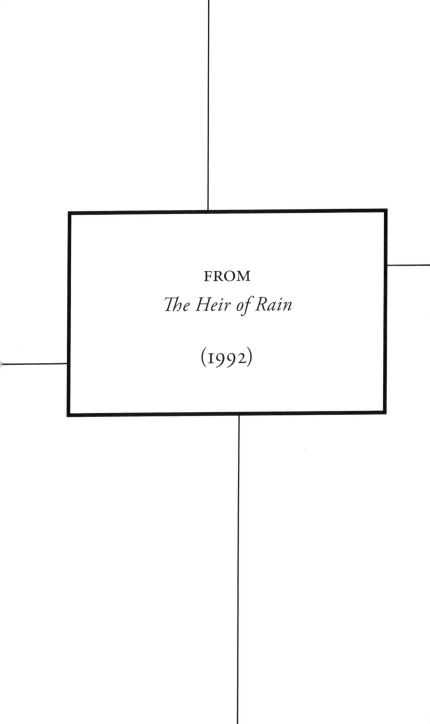

FROM

The Heir of Rain

(1992)

Two-legged grasses, the faces visible,
draw near to the four walls of my home.
They offer a kiss to the *mezuzah* and shuffle
into my bed where I murmur: Take pity
winged pain, reveal your genius
of incising poison into thoughts, memories,
where there is only a bitter spark—fanning it into flames.

Do you bring fresh news, two-legged grasses?

Two-legged grasses, solve me this puzzle:
Does anyone take pleasure when iron-combs
cut up the body together with the soul?
Who takes pleasure in such a harvest?
Just a moment more, just a moment,
my last query:
Should I leave my inheritance to you?

The two-legged grasses bow devoutly.

1988

צוווייפֿיסיקע גראָזן, די פֿנימלעך קעניטיקע,
דערענענטערן זיך צו מײַן היים די פֿירװוענטיקע.
דערלאַנגען אַ קוש די מזוזה און שאַרן זיך
אַרײַן צו מײַן בעט װי איך מורמל: דערבאַרעם זיך
באַפֿליגלטער װײַטיק, אַנטפֿלעק דײַן גאָונות
פֿון אײַנציינדלען סם אין געדאַנקען, זכרונות,
אַװו נאָר אַ ביטערער פֿונק—אים צעבלאָזן.

צי ברענגט איר אַ בשׂורה, צװווייפֿיסיקע גראָזן?

צוווייפֿיסיקע גראָזן, באַשיידט מיר די רעטעניש:
צי האָט װער הנאה װען איבזיערנע קאַמען
צעשינדן דעם גוף מיט נשמה צוזאַמען?
פֿאַר װעמען די פֿרייד פֿון אַזאַ מין גערעטעניש?
אַ װײלע, אַ װײלע,
מײַן לעצטינקע שאלה:
צי זאָל איך אַצינד מײַן ירושה אײַך לאָזן?

פֿאַרנײַגן זיך פֿרום די צוווייפֿיסיקע גראָזן.

1988

Like Sun through a Crevice

I love a human being not yet born: Perhaps he will
be born on earth a hundred years from now
or somewhere in a strange time of perfect nothing
and he—the one and only to complete the zeros.

I see that one not yet born like sun through a crevice,
and have a name for him and have faith in him.
There is a silence between the two of us that we both
     understand
and a love for the beauty of that silence between the two of us.

I write these lines to one not yet born. To that someone
whom I am ready to step through hell with.
It can be that one who is not yet born loves me from long ago
and our doubleheart has never ceased to beat and make its
     claim.

I see a person who is not yet born. Were lions
to howl me into the dust, I would not cease believing
in that unborn, in that silence the two of us both understand,
both loving the beauty of that silence between the two of us.

1989

ווי זון דורך אַ שפּאַרונע

כ'האָב ליב אַ ניט־געבוירענעם בן־אָדם: אפֿשר וועט ער
געבוירן ווערן אויף דער ערד מיט אַ יאָרהונדערט שפּעטער
צי ערגעץ אין אַן אויסטערלישער צײַט פֿון לויטער נולן
און ער—אַן איינס אַן איינציקער די נולן צו פֿאַרפֿולן.

איך זע דעם ניט־געבוירענעם, ווי זון דורך אַ שפּאַרונע,
איך האָב פֿאַר אים אַ נאָמען און איך האָב אין אים אמונה.
פֿאַראַן אַ שוויגן צווישן ביידן וואָס מיר צוויי פֿאַרשטייען
און האָבן ליב די שיינקייט פֿון דער שווײַגעניש אין צווייען.

איך שרײַב די שורות צו אַ ניט־געבוירענעם. צו יענעם
וואָס בינען בין איך גרייט מיט אים צו שפּאַנען דורכן גיהנום.
קאָן זײַן, דער ניט־געבוירענער האָט ליב מיך פֿון לאַנגאַנען
און ס'הערט ניט אויף צו קלאַפֿן אונדזער טאָפּלהאַרץ און מאָנען.

איך זע אַ מענטשן וואָס איז ניט־געבוירן. זאָלן לײַבן
צעברומען מיך אויף שטויב, איך וועל ניט אויפֿהערן צו גלייבן
אין אומגעבוירענעם, אין שווײַגן וואָס מיר צוויי פֿאַרשטייען
און האָבן ליב די שיינקייט פֿון דער שווײַגעניש אין צווייען.

1989

Poem about Nothing

A window remained. No wall. No glass. No nothing.
But also the window remains only in my memory.
A diamond that has cut out glass from absolutely nothing.
So I should catch a sign that I am alive—from the sixth floor.

A sign that I am alive and am the master of absolutely nothing,
I blow breath into me and a quiver permeates me.
From the sixth floor, eye to eye, I converse with nothingness:
We are two, the devil behind us is the third one.

A pleasure to sense that I am the master of nothingness,
my window not-there radiating like the dawn.
From the sixth floor I see how that nothingness crumbles into
    dust,
and there is no one in whose pockets he can hide.

Only a window remained. No wall. No glass. No nothing.
But only in my memory there is a house. A window.
From the sixth floor I see: That nothingness turns away
    from me,
who attacked me like a gangster with a knife.

1990

ליד וועגן גאָרנישט

געבליבן איז אַ פֿענצטער. אָן אַ וואַנט. אָן גלאָז. אָן גאָרנישט.
נאָר אויך דער פֿענצטער איז געבליבן בלויז אין מײַן זכּרון.
אַ דימענט האָט עס אויסגעשניטן גלאָז פֿון גאָלע גאָרנישט,
איך זאָל דערזען אַ סימן אַז איך לעב—פֿון זעקסטן גאָרן.

אַ סימן אַז איך לעב און בין אין דער האַר פֿון גאָלע גאָרנישט,
אַ בלאָז אַרײַן מײַן אָטעם און סע נעמט אַדורך אַ ציטער.
פֿון זעקסטן גאָרן, אויג אויף אויג, איך שמועס מיטן גאָרנישט:
מיר זענען צוויי, דער טײַוול הינטער בײַדן איז דער דריטער.

אַ תּענוג צו דערפֿילן, אַז איך בין דער האַר פֿון גאָרנישט,
מײַן פֿענצטער וואָס איז ניט פֿאַראַן באַגינענדיק צעשטראַלט זיך.
פֿון זעקסטן גאָרן זע איך, ווי ס׳צעפֿאַלט אין שטויב דער גאָרנישט,
ניטאָ איז קיינער וואָס אין זײַנע קעשענעס באַהאַלט זיך.

געבליבן בלויז אַ פֿענצטער אָן אַ וואַנט. אָן גלאָז. אָן גאָרנישט.
נאָר בלויז אין מײַן זכּרון איז פֿאַראַן אַ שטוב. אַ פֿענצטער.
פֿון זעקסטן גאָרן זע איך: ס׳טוט זיך אָפּ פֿון מיר דער גאָרנישט,
וואָס מיט אַ מעסער איז ער מיך באַפֿאַלן ווי אַ גענגסטער.

1990

237

I Seek Those Few People Who
to This Day Remember My Mother

It follows that while my mother lived, I lived as a result;
I couldn't imagine: Some day she would cease to be.
And in the winter her shawl became a meadow
where cold stars warmed my bones.

My Jewish mother-city, in one-two-three, became a shambles.
My cherry tree in the window laughed with black buds.
I hid in the folds of the shawl
when a scythe mowed over me.

I hid from that golden carrion
the sun. She too wanted to capture me.
And in the winter the shawl became a meadow
where my mother's prayerful sounds protected me.

I seek those few, no more
than you can count on the fingers of one hand,
who to this day remember my mother, her shawl—
may they live to become younger.
It follows that because my mother lived, I have lived,
and in the winter her shawl became a meadow.

July 28, 1991

איך זוך די ווינציקע, וואָס ביז
אַצינד געדענקען זיי מיין מאַמען

בשעת מיין מאַמע האָט געלעבט, געלעבט האָב איך במילא,
האָב ניט געקענט זיך פֿאָרשטעלן: זי וועט אַ מאָל ניט ווערן.
און ווינטערצייט געוואָרן איז אַ לאָנקע איר פֿאַטשיילע
ווי ס'ווארעמען די ביינער קאַלטע שטערן.

מיין עיר-ואם געוואָרן איז אַ איינס-צווייי אַ שבֿרי-כלי.
מיין קאָרשנבוים אין פֿענצטער האָט געלאַקט מיט שוואַרצע בליטן.
איך האָב זיך אויסבאַהאַלטן אין די קניטשן פֿון פֿאַטשיילע
ווען איבער מיר געגאַנגען איז אַ קאַסע און געשניטן.

איך האָב זיך אויסבאַהאַלטן פֿון דער גילדענער נבֿלה
די זון. זי אויכעט האָט געוואָלט מיך פֿאַנגגען.
און ווינטערצייט געוואָרן איז אַ לאָנקע די פֿאַטשיילע
ווי ס'האָבן מיך באַשיצט מיין מאַמעס תּפֿילהדיקע קלאַנגען.

איך זוך די ווינציקע,
ניט מער: ווי פֿון אַ האַנט די פֿינגער,
וואָס ביז אַצינד געדענקען זיי מיין מאַמען, איר פֿאַטשיילע,
דערלעבן זאָלן זיי צו ווערן יינגער,
ווייל ווען מיין מאַמע האָט געלעבט האָב איך געלעבט במילא
און ווינטערצייט געוואָרן איז אַ לאָנקע איר פֿאַטשיילע.

28סטן יולי 1991

239

Soon it will happen!
The black rings
become tight and tighter around my throat!
Impersonal, like a cobblestone,
I will remain lying under hoofs,
redeemed from the world;
but in my depth
three ants will remain wandering:
One,
under laurels of my childhood,
will return to magic-forest.
The second,
under shield of my dream,
will return to dream-land;
and the third,
the one that carries my word,
won't have anywhere to go
because the land of credible words
is infected,
and she will stand guard
in the valley of shadows
alone and lonely
over my remains.

באַלד וועט עס געשען!
די שוואַרצע רינגען
ווערן ענג און ענגער אַרום האַלדז!
אומפערזענלעך, ווי אַ שטיין אין ברוק
וועל איך בלײַבן ליגן אונטער טלאָען
אויסגעלײזט פֿון וועלט:
נאָר אין מײַן טיף
וועלן בלײַבן וואַגלען דרײַ מוראַשקעס:
איינע,
אונטער לאָרבער פֿון מײַן קינדשאַפֿט,
וועט זיך אומקערן אין כּישוף־וואַלד.
צווייטע,
אונטער פֿאַנצער פֿון מײַן חלום,
וועט זיך אומקערן אין חלום־לאַנד;
און די דריטע
די וואָס טראָגט מײַן וואָרט,
וועט קיין וועג ניט האָבן,
ווײַל פֿאַרפעסטיקט
איז דאָס לאַנד פֿון גלײביבנדיקע ווערטער,
וועט זי וואַכן אינעם טאָל פֿון שאַטנס
איין און עלנט
איבער מײַן געביין.

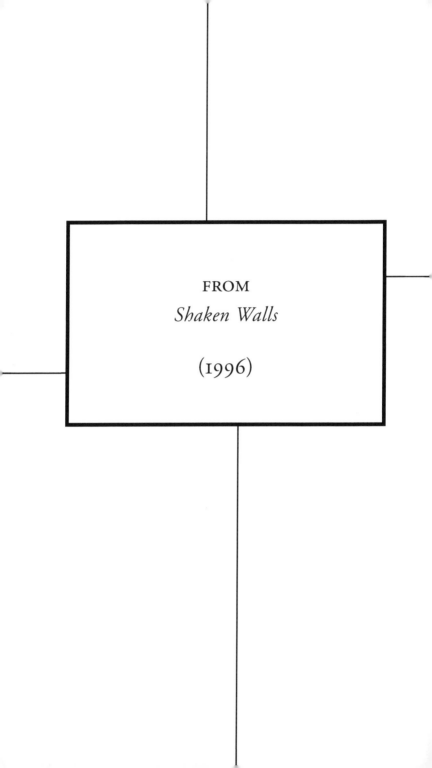

FROM
Shaken Walls

(1996)

Just before his bar mitzvah a boyhood friend of mine, Leybeleh,
tried to hang himself. No one knew if he was serious or joking.
Maybe the boy thought: Hanging oneself is a good deed—
      a mitzvah!
But his angel cut him down from the belt
and rescued him from hanging.

And Leybeleh grew up overnight. He
fled to Paris,
fled torpor and stricture.

When we met, a mirror grew startled:
Instead of a Leybeleh an old man suddenly turned up,
with quite a name
in the secrets of atoms.

Something was itching me to ask what
made him hang himself back then: A girl? First love?

And when later on I accompanied him to the plane,
that curiosity shot out from my mute tongue.

And that boy and famous man answered:
"Back then the beginning of a drama was hatching in me,
a passion to catch a glimpse of death—my very first
unique atomic encounter."

מײַן ייִנגל-חבֿר לײַבעלע האָט ערבֿ זײַן בר-מיצווה
געפרוּווט זיך צו ענגאַגען. קיינער וווייס ניט: ערנסט אָדער שפּאַסיק.
ס׳קען זײַן, דער ייִנגל האָט געטראַכט: זיך ענגאַגען איז אַ מיצווה!
זײַן מלאך האָט אים אָבער אָפּגעשניטן פונעם פאַסיק
און אויסגעלייזט פֿון הענגעניש.

און לײַבעלע איז אויסגעוואַקסן איבער נאַכט. ער איז
אַנטרונען קיין פּאַריז
פֿון הינערפלעט און ענגעניש.

בשעת מיר האָבן זיך באַגעגנט האָט אַ שפּיגל זיך דערשראָקן:
אַנשטאָט אַ לײַבעלע פאַיִאַווועט פלוצעם זיך אַ זקן
און גאָר אַ וואָשנער נאָמען
אין די סודות פֿון אַטאָמען.

ס׳האָט ווער געצוויגן מיר די צונג צו פֿרעגן אים די סיבה
פֿון זײַן אַמאָליק הענגענען זיך: אַ מיידל? ערשטע ליבע?

און אַז איך האָב אים שפּעטער צו באַגלייט צום עראָפּלאַן,
אַרויסגעריסן האָט זיך פֿון מײַן שטומער צונג די פֿרעגעניש.

און ס׳האָט געענטפֿערט מיר דער ייִנגל און באַרימטער מאַן:
ס׳האָט יעמאָלט זיך געפיקט זיך מיר אין דער אָנהייב פֿון אַ דראַמע:
אַ תּשוקה צו דערזען דעם טויט—מײַן סאַמע
ערשטמאָליקסטע אַטאָמישע באַגעגעניש.

A special announcement: The Yiddish Word
has severed itself from the globe, from the power
to attract even more victims to its sacrificial altar.

The Yiddish Word now moves
among the planets
just as a blink of an eye ago
it did among the Pleiades
of Yiddish poets
anointed on earth.

The Yiddish Word now moves
above over-above
and warms up millions of cold particles of dust.
It can recognize in them the singers and sayers
who back then in the blink of an eye
marched, hymned.

And the Yiddish Word gazes down
into abysses and foundations.
The globe below is not bigger
than a diamond set in a ring.

אַן עקסטרע מעלדונג: ס'האָט זיך אָפּגעריסן
דאָס יידיש־וואָרט פֿון ערדקויל, פֿונעם כּוח
אַלץ מער קרבנות צוצוציִען צו איר ערד־מזבח,

דאָס יידיש־וואָרט באַוועגט זיך איצטער
צווישן די פּלאַנעטן
אַזוי ווי מיט אַן אויגפֿינטל צוריק
צווישן פּלעיאַדעס
אויף דר׳ערד געזאַלבטע
יידישע פּאָעטן.

דאָס יידיש־וואָרט באַוועגט זיך איצטער
אויבן־איבער־אויבן
און וואַרעמט אָן מיליִאָנען קאַלטע שטויבן.
ס'דערקענט אין זיי די זינגערס און די זאָגערס,
וואָס האָבן מיט אַן אויגפֿינטל צוריק
מאַרשירט, געהימענט.

און ס'קוקט אַראָפּ דאָס יידיש־וואָרט
צו אָפּגרונטן און גרונטן:
די ערדקויל אונטן איז ניט גרעסער ווי אין
אַ פֿינגערל אַ דימענט.

It sometimes seems to me the world
will endure because somewhere a lucky fugitive
lives and my mother is lodged
in his memory's eye.

I will clothe myself in white thorns,
wander
and seek and find that man of memory,
and wallow like a deaf mute in his dust,
and will bless him.

און דאַכטן דאַכט מיר: ס׳האָט נאָך וועלט אַ קיום,
ווײל ערגעץ לעבט אַ מזלדיק אַנטרונענער
וואָס אינעם שוואַרצאַפּל פֿון זײן זכרון
איז אײנגעפֿאַסט מײן מאַמע.

כ׳וועל אָנטאָן זיך אין ווײסע דערנער,
וואַנדערן
און זוכן און געפֿינען דעם געדענקער,
שטויבן זיך אַ שטומער אין זײן שטויב
און וועל אים בענטשן.

All that is past, experienced, previous,
now floats through me and through my temples
like twilight clouds, in order
to re-live what was outlived,
and to see again what was seen:
May I truthfully sense my world
and weigh it in the balance
before my hands become vacant . . .

Come closer, my friends,
I want to thank you and bless you:
Your divine drops
that have healed my vexation,
that have given light and will not cease
to give light.

אַל דאָס געוועזענע, איבערגעלעבטע, אַמאָליקע,
שוועבט מיר אַדורך דורך די שלייפֿן אַצינד
ווי פֿאַרנאַכטיקע וואָלקנס, כדי
איבערצולעבן דאָס איבערגעלעבטע
און זען דאָס געזעענע ווידער:
אמתדיק זאָל איך דערפֿילן מײַן וועלט
און זי מישפטן
איידער די העגט ווערן ליידיק . . .

נעענטער, מײַנע חבֿרים,
אײַך וויל איך דאַנקען און בענטשן.
איר געטלעכע טראָפּנס
וואָס האָבן געהיילט מײַן גריזאָטע,
וואָס האָבן געלויכטן און וועלן ניט אויפֿהערן
לײַכטן.

I know that nothing remains of my sister except her name
and that I am the one and only who remembers her name.
So I don't need to write letters addressed to her
and call an unknown girl by her name.

I myself have given her food with a shovel,
a black challah that was dug out by my shovel.
Only, my sister wasn't satisfied, so my shovel
gave her a second black challah. Ask the shovel.

And though I know my sister is on the other side of life
I am not separated from my living sister,
and when I am hungry—she comes as a glowing revelation
and lets me take a little bite of her black challah.

איך ווייס אַז פֿון מײַן שוועסטער איז געבליבן בלויז איר נאָמען
און אַז איך בין דער אײנציק־אײנער וואָס געדענקט איר נאָמען.
באַדאַרף איך דאָך ניט שרײַבן בריוו צו איר און אויף איר נאָמען
און אָנרופֿן אַן אומבאַקאַנטער מײדל מיט איר נאָמען.

איך האָב איר דאָך אַלײן געגעבן עסן מיט אַ רידל
אַ שוואַרצע חלה וואָס אַרויסגעצויגן האָט מײַן רידל.
נאָר זאַטער איז מײַן שוועסטער ניט געוואָרן, האָט מײַן רידל
אַ צווייטע שוואַרצע חלה איר געגעבן. פֿרעג דעם רידל.

און כאַטש איך ווייס: אויף יענער זײַט פֿון לעבן איז מײַן שוועסטער—
ניט אָפּגעזונדערט בין איך פֿון מײַן לעבעדיקער שוועסטער.
און אַז כ׳בין הונגעריק—זי ווערט אַ ליכטיקע נתגלה
און לאָזט מיר אויך אַ קלײנעם ביס טאָן פֿון איר שוואַרצער חלה.

253

I regret that I was born
when people wanted to stone me to death.
I regret that I died
and no one was there to mourn for me.

I regret that my first line—
written in the dark with a pencil
and the world-beginning it created—
was made of paper and not of fire.

I regret that I did not flesh out from my own body
an heir for my grandfather.
Regret that I did not draw out
from his closed mouth the Ineffable Name.

1993–1994

חרטה האָב איך וואָס איך בין געבוירן
ווען מענטשן האָבן מיך געוואָלט פֿאַרשטיינען.
חרטה האָב איך וואָס איך בין געשטאָרבן
און קיינער איז ניטאָ מיך צו באַוויינען.

חרטה האָב איך וואָס מײַן ערשטע שורה
געשריבן אין דער פֿינצטער מיט אַ בלײַער
און וואָס מײַן אָנהייב־וועלט זי האָט באַשאַפֿן—
געווען איז פֿון פּאַפּיר און ניט פֿון פֿײַער.

חרטה האָב איך וואָס איך האָב מײַן זיידן
פֿון אייגן לײַב ניט אויסגעפֿלייישט קיין יורש.
חרטה, וואָס כ׳האָב ניט אַרויסגעצויגן
פֿון זײַן פֿאַרמאַכטן מויל דעם שם־המפֿורש.

1994–1993

SPORADIC VISITANT. . .

After Avrom Sutzkever's last poem in *Twin Brother*

— RICHARD J. FEIN

Sporadic Visitant . . .

Sporadic visitant,
release
sounds, impressions
confined within me,
tongs or tweezers
plucking them out of me

Sporadic visitant,
outsource my sources,
assume whatever forms agree with you,
reach in as far back as you need,
as long as you transfer what you grip,
I stronger from the strongest pain,
stronger from the first love,
stronger from the last love,
as you pry, clutch and issue

Sporadic visitant,
perhaps you are the Tree of Life
extending its limbs towards me
outside the window
so I can reach and touch a twig,
the tree giving forth from its innerness,
trusting its textures from trunk to tip,
containing epitomes of forest,
my own mind foraging in the brush of itself

Sporadic visitant,
Sutzkever's figments of Yiddish,
Genesis-Tree of speech:
Vines sinuating on branches,
sky punctuating leaves,
lichens modifying wood

Sporadic visitant—
translate me
translating Sutzkever

(RJF)

AFTERWORD

Sent to *Siberia*

THROUGH MY TRANSLATING IT, SUTZKEVER'S *SIBERIA* BECAME closer to me than it was in all my rereadings of the poem, this gift of translation, where writing is a form of possessing another poem. In translating you sense more deeply than ever the full weight of every punctuation mark in the poem. The translator becomes the author of the poem in his own language, akin to the original maker of the poem. The translator works his way to a "second original," as Yankev Glatshteyn called Yehoash's Yiddish translation of the Hebrew Bible.

Becoming attuned to *Siberia*, I absorbed the sounds and the words and the child's responses in the poem. I entered the world Sutzkever had entered previously. As my friend Teresa Iverson pointed out to me, in writing *Siberia* Sutzkever had to learn that in a child-adult way he

> must have a mind of winter
> To regard the frost and the boughs
> Of the pine-trees crusted with snow . . .
> (Wallace Stevens, "The Snow Man")

Or, as Sutzkever imagined it,

> the artist Frost paints on my skull,
> as on a windowpane, its colorful snow legends.

261

As translator, I sense myself the maker of a new version—in English. Translating Yiddish poetry is doing my own work. However (and it's a truth that makes me uncomfortable), I must confess that sometimes in translating Yiddish poetry I have felt I was putting off, even avoiding, the writing of my own poems. And I might lurch between these sensations of dedication and avoidance as I kept working at putting Yiddish into English. I wondered, Could both senses be right?. I hatch out of my contradictions.

At times there is a pleasure in turning a Yiddish passage into English because I am led into a rhythm and phrasing I hadn't sensed in my work before, as in translating Sutzkever's "To My Father" (from *Siberia*) about his father's burial:

> When the heartbeat of the pickaxe
> hacked out your new hut, abyss
> that swallowed you up where
> you still glitter under the ice,
> I wanted to fall in there with you!

There is a terse beat here, a synchronization of sounds, indeed a finely cut sentence, I don't think I would have reached without Sutzkever prompting me there. Sutzkever's world of Siberia—its images and the child's response—drew us both into poetry. Sutzkever could show me how to shape my poetry just as his Siberia led him into poetry. Renato Poggioli affirms in his ample essay "The Added Artificer" (a great sanction of my efforts), "[L]ike the original poet, the translator is a Narcissus who in this case chooses to contemplate his own likeness not in the spring of nature but in the pool of art."

In *Siberia* Sutzkever offers us the Jewish boy not as a *kheyder yingl*, a Hebrew school child, but as a little pagan—*Siberia* is Sutzkever's *The Rite of Spring*. It is a Jewish child's fascination with primitiveness—the source of the poem. Even the rituals of another people (the Kyrgyz) can invigorate his imagination and that of the later young poet writing the poem. Those early years are what Sutzkever draws on some two decades later in Vilna, where he composes the poem. The invigoration of the child's mind leads to the vigor of Sutzkever's Yiddish, which in turn further prompts the child's sensations.

Sex and death are not the only greatest themes of poetry (as Yeats would have it), for childhood is another of its great themes. The child in *Siberia* is touched by the sun and the ice and the river (frozen, and then breaking up). They open him up to a new realm:

> I a child turn into an avalanche
> whom light and wonder shaped.

The abstraction of the second line is shocked into action by the jolting image of the preceding line.

Siberia in Sutzkever's *Siberia* puts the child in touch with Genesis-like powers as the landscape works on him. That landscape breeds a sensual immediacy in the child's mind, affecting Sutzkever's Yiddish. One of his favorite words is *b'reyshisdik*— Genesis (*b'reyshis*) turned adjectival through the adding of a suffix, *dik*. Prefixes and suffixes make for a formational richness in Yiddish (e.g., prefixes neatly turning nouns into verbs), and Sutzkever's bent for neologisms (sometimes excessively so) is encouraged by the morphology of Yiddish. The world is not only there to be described but language is also there to give birth to itself. But with *b'reyshisdik* in particular Sutzkever wants to touch a condition of wonder—a divine-like preservation you might say he wants to incorporate in himself—prominent in his early work to his Holocaust poems to his ingenious poems of self-study. That late book, *Twin Brother*, Sutzkever's masterpiece, is, I think, the book of his I most admire. *Siberia* is the book of his I adore. Reading it also thrills me in the way poetry can—as its language incites us to new crevices of experience. Sutzkever is a master of homeopathy in his poetry—to allow the self to be touched by a destructive element so as to survive it in its even worse form.

There is a glow of wonder around the works of this "last great Yiddish poet" (that sad *de rigueur* label inevitably pinned on him), who was also a partisan during World War II, that enjoins the responsive reader not to reduce the marvels of Sutzkever's observations, the transformations of landscape and language, the sprite of sensations, the rich eeriness, to the dulled triumph of "the national poet of Yiddish."

Not to read Yiddish poetry to be an expert; not to read Yiddish poetry as part of an effort to enter Yiddish culture; not even to read Yiddish poetry because I love the language—but to read Yiddish poetry because I need to, just as it is necessary for me to write my own poetry. And through the Yiddish poem I find sounds and worlds carved into the still uncanny shapes on the page, yet shapes I saw in childhood, shapes that puzzled me and that also were inside of me. And translation puts me back in touch with this language, as a kind of child-adult. And perhaps with luck I can also transform these Yiddish powers for purposes in my own poems. I am indebted to Rosanna Warren for the delicious notion that for the poet translation is a way of supplementing his vitamin deficiencies. Translating Sutzkever, especially *Siberia*, furthered me as a poet, particularly in the refining of imagery.

May those Yiddish shapes and sounds take me deeper, further. May they not become for me a specialty, an ethnic identity, a homage to the past, to the dead. May they never become a skill for me. Oh, Yiddish letters, may you ever retain the otherness of your shapes I work at absorbing. Oh, Yiddish letters, retain your quiver on the page, in my ear. Oh, Yiddish letters, continue to draw me into yourselves, as if childhood puzzlement, embarrassment, and annoyance over you and your sounds grow within me into something greater, as if fears and confusions and rejections of childhood can become the source of poetry for the adult. Yiddish, I must still get to know you as I must get to know myself. And the deepest way I can get to know you is by translating you as you are shaped into poetry.

How Yiddish, in the very shape of its letters, can take me more deeply into English—my English—is one of the great jujitsu moves of my life, that intrusively claiming Yiddish that made its way into the deepest loculi of my life and writing. Every Yiddish poet I have ever translated has been a psychopomp for me, leading me into depths where the sounds of Yiddish become the shades I must meet. And Yiddish thereby becomes a stand-in for what I earlier rejected in myself and now engage. If, as the famous poet advised, I must change my life, then you might say I did so (or tried to) by learning Yiddish.

YIDDISH POETS SPEAK TO ME FROM THE GRAVE

> Translate us
> as if you were returning
> to your childhood,
> as if you'd missed it
> and now find it—a gift
> age has given you.
> Translate us,
> as if you'd postponed
> your own life
> and just now return to it,
> happy to find
> that nothing
> can keep you from us.
> When you go down,

when you visit us,
walk where you feared to go.
We will speak Yiddish,
our words shaking off
the darkness and gathering
around you. We will
be patient.
Only now, Ruvn,
only now,
do you know
how long
we've been waiting
for you,
above and below.

To enter Yiddish and transform it into English has become
one of my tasks. To translate Yiddish is a kind of frottage for
me, in the sexual sense of that word. I want Sutzkever's meta-
phor-making powers to rub off on me, as if I were also drawing
powers from the strange charactery and utterance of Yiddish that
infused my childhood:

And your very first dream visits you in a dream,
and your very last dream is pledged to the first one.
(Sutzkever, "Not even the least of things . . ." in
Twin Brother)

I am drawn to Ruth Wisse's remarks about the teaching
and presentation of Yiddish: "The priorities will be an outcome
of your deepest needs. In other words, what do you need from
Yiddish literature? What do you need it to provide you with?"

I had enjoyed reading *Siberia* for years—I returned to the
cycle more than to any other group of Sutzkever's poems—but

never felt the urge to translate any of the poems from the cycle. I kept on enjoying them from time to time. After Sutzkever died in January 2010, I read *Siberia* again (homage!). And I wondered why I still felt no need to translate it. That winter I read the cycle two more times, yet still, to my puzzlement, felt no need to translate it. (Was I afraid of abandoning my own poems?) "Let me read it once more," I said to myself in March and somehow the ice broke and I felt called upon to translate a few poems from the cycle. And then eventually I had to do the whole thing. Now translating *Siberia* was to be part of my work. Yet, as I have acknowledged, to my discomfort, sometimes translation can feel like a substitute for my own poetry. Maybe that's when compulsion to translate threatens to turn into mere obligation to finish the job. But if that job is really yours, the details will come back to stir you.

Sutzkever is not as dear to me as several other Yiddish poets: Yankev Glatshteyn, Moyshe-Leyb Halpern, H. Leivick. But *Siberia* was different from their work in its concentration on the growth of the child's mind and the birth of the poet. His *Siberia* turned out to be closer to my early years in Brooklyn and their resultant poetry than I initially recognized. It's as if the shapes of nature that haunted Sutzkever's child turned into the shapes of Yiddish that lurked in me as a child. It's as if each Yiddish letter was carved by a coping saw. Finally, Sutzkever's poems became for me

> The marker-paws some animal
> had sown like roses in the snow . . .

Translating (or traversing) *Siberia* I felt myself entering a luster I had not sensed in my own poems. And the illogic of his language could both grip and puzzle me—as when he says to the snowman: "near you my dream stands kneeling." Sutzkever compelled me to keep the contradictory position though I couldn't explain or justify it to myself. I waited for clarity to visit me but couldn't hold off the translation until it arrived. It was as if I were both standing and kneeling (as well as sitting!) before his phrases. His Yiddish world eventually revealed itself to me, entered me. The body of Sutzkever's poems, his Yiddish, invigorated the body of my translations, my English.

In writing my poem to Sutzkever, "Sporadic visitant . . .," the last poem I include in this book, I found myself several times looking around for the Yiddish original, so I could check my translation against that "original." I was both standing in my own poem and looking for the ur-Yiddish. Aha! It comes to me as I write these very words, Sutzkever's "near you my dream stands kneeling" makes use of the way the snowman both stands and seems planted in the snow.

In translating *Siberia* I felt I was reaching for or returning to the source of poetry, a child's imagination as evoked by the poet discovering his themes and words:

> A fresh dazzle on the branches
> exhales wolf howls.

> * * *

> The sun sets in me. The sun—no more.
> Only its fiery pelt is seen
> on a long branch. And I—speechless—
> want to put it on before it dies away.

> * * *

> A harrow cuts through damp clouds
> and opens their secrets.

The child knew a wonder, and the poet knows a power.

NOTES

"THE BURIAL," PG. 70–72

Zaretshe cemetery: Main Jewish cemetery in Vilna before and at the time of World War II.

minyan: A quorum of ten Jews (traditionally men) needed for a religious service.

kheyder: Elementary Hebrew school. The first time a very young child is brought to *kheyder*, he might be carried and literally handed over to the teacher.

Gabriel: In Jewish mysticism, the archangel Gabriel is associated with gold. He also appears to the prophet Daniel and reveals to him what his visions mean (Daniel 8:16–27; 9:21-27).

Sewer: Some Jews escaped the Vilna Ghetto through its sewers.

"A POEM WITHOUT A NAME," PG. 92–93

bruder (Yiddish): Brother.

"[GATHER ME . . .,]" PG. 96–97

siddur: Jewish prayer book.

H. Leivick (1888–1962): A well-known Yiddish poet in New York who suffered a stroke and became paralyzed and speechless in his last four years.

Sambation: A tempestuous river of Jewish legend preventing exiles from returning to the Promised Land. It calmed only on the Sabbath, when Jews aren't permitted to travel. The river became a symbol of Jewish exile.

"[NOT ONE, NOT TWO . . .,]" PG. 218–220

In the Bible, counting people one by one, as in a census, is to court danger from evil forces and to offend God (see Exodus 30:11–12; 2 Samuel, 24:10). The custom arose among Jews to count people by saying, "Not one, not two, etc."

"[TWO-LEGGED GRASSES . . .,]" PG. 232–233

mezuzah: A small piece of parchment imprinted with a Biblical passage and rolled up into a container affixed to a doorframe at the entrance of a house or apartment indicating that a Jewish family lives herein. The container is kissed with one's fingers as one enters the apartment or house.

Made in the USA
Monee, IL
18 August 2023